The
HIDDEN PLACES
of
HEREFORDSHIRE, WORCESTERSHIRE & SHROPSHIRE

D1465148

Edited by
Peter Long

Published by:
Travel Publishing Ltd
7a Apollo House, Calleva Park
Aldermaston, Berks, RG7 8TN

ISBN 1-902-00736-0

© Travel Publishing Ltd 1999

First Published:	*1992*		*Fourth Edition:*	*1999*
Second Edition:	*1995*			
Third Edition:	*1997*			

Regional Titles in the Hidden Places Series:

Cambridgeshire & Lincolnshire   Channel Islands
Cheshire   Chilterns
Cornwall   Devon
Dorset, Hants & Isle of Wight   Essex
Gloucestershire   Heart of England
Hereford, Worcs & Shropshire   Highlands & Islands
Kent   Lake District & Cumbria
Lancashire   Norfolk
Northeast Yorkshire   Northumberland & Durham
North Wales   Nottinghamshire
Peak District   Potteries
Somerset   South Wales
Suffolk   Surrey
Sussex   Thames Valley
Warwickshire & W Midlands   Wiltshire
Yorkshire Dales

National Titles in the Hidden Places Series:

England   Ireland
Scotland   Wales

Printing by: Ashford Press, Gosport
Maps by: © MAPS IN MINUTES ™ (1998)
Line Drawings: Caroline Hounsham
Editor: Peter Long
Cover Design: Lines & Words, Aldermaston
Cover Photographs: Malvern Hills, Worcestershire; The Iron Bridge, Shropshire; Ross-on-Wye, Herefordshire. © Britain on View/Stockwave.

All information is included by the publishers in good faith and is believed to be correct at the time of going to press. No responsibility can be accepted for errors.

FOREWORD

The Hidden Places series is a collection of easy to use travel guides taking you, in this instance, on a relaxed but informative tour of Herefordshire, Worcestershire and Shropshire - three counties with differing characters. Worcestershire is a county of rich, fruit-bearing, fertile lowlands through which flow the rivers Avon and Severn, and characterised by stone farms and black and white timber houses. Herefordshire, on the other hand, is a wooded, undulating county with a plethora of interesting small villages and hamlets and pleasant country lanes. Shropshire has recently been accorded the title of *"The most romantic county in Britain"*, has a rich industrial heritage as well as beautiful countryside and is full of stately homes, attractive gardens and many other visitor attractions.

Our books contain a wealth of interesting information on the history, the countryside, the towns and villages and the more established places of interest in the counties. But they also promote the more secluded and little known visitor attractions and places to stay, eat and drink many of which are easy to miss unless you know exactly where you are going.

We include hotels, inns, restaurants, public houses, teashops, various types of accommodation, historic houses, museums, gardens, garden centres, craft centres and many other attractions throughout Herefordshire, Worcestershire and Shropshire, all of which are comprehensively indexed. Most places have an attractive line drawing and are cross-referenced to coloured maps found at the rear of the book. We do not award merit marks or rankings but concentrate on describing the more interesting, unusual or unique features of each place with the aim of making the reader's stay in the local area an enjoyable and stimulating experience.

Whether you are visiting the area for business or pleasure or in fact are living in the counties we do hope that you enjoy reading and using this book. We are always interested in what readers think of places covered (or not covered) in our guides so please do not hesitate to use the reader reaction forms provided to give us your considered comments. We also welcome any general comments which will help us improve the guides themselves. Finally if you are planning to visit any other corner of the British Isles we would like to refer you to the list of other *Hidden Places* titles to be found at the rear of the book.

CONTENTS

1 South Herefordshire & the Wye Valley

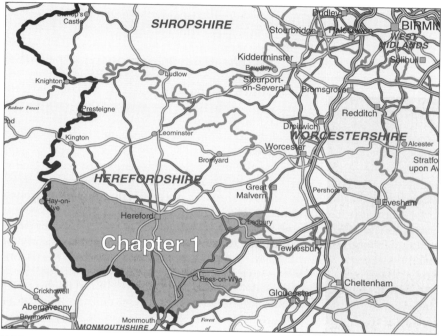

© MAPS IN MINUTES ™ (1998)

"Wherever one goes, there will not be a mile that is visually unrewarding." Sir Nikolaus Pevsner was clearly impressed, and today's visitors will also find delights at every turn in the rolling landscape, the pretty villages and the charming market towns. Herefordshire had few natural resources, so the industrial scars that spoil many counties are mercifully absent; the beauty remains relatively intact, so too the peace, and motorists will generally find jam-free roads. Apples and hops are the traditional crops of Herefordshire, and the cider industry is still a thriving one. The days when almost every farm produced its own cider are long gone, but many of the old mills are preserved on the farms or in museums. 9,500 acres of the county are given over to cider orchards, and 63 million gallons of cider are produced here each year - well over half the UK total. In western Herefordshire perry is something of a speciality, the drink being made on similar lines to cider but with pears instead of apples. Hops have been cultivated in the county since the 16th century and once provided late summer work for thousands of pickers,

mainly from the Black Country and South Wales. The industry is considerably smaller than before, and mechanisation has greatly reduced the need for human effort. The poles and wires are a less common sight than previously, but they can still be seen, along with the occasional kiln for drying the hops - the Herefordshire equivalent of Kent's oast houses. Among the animals, sheep and cattle are a familiar sight; Hereford cattle still abound, and their stock are now to be found in many parts of the world, particularly the Americas. Industry was never developed to any great extent, partly through the remoteness of the location and the poverty of communications, and the visible traces of the county's heritage are confined largely to castles (this is Border territory) and churches. The castles were mainly of the straightforward motte and bailey variety, the motte being a tower-topped earthen mound surrounded by a small court, the bailey a larger yard with the stables and workshops and accommodation. Skirmishes with the Welsh were a common occurrence for many centuries, and one of the county's best-known landmarks, Offa's Dyke, was built in the 8th century as a defence against the marauders.

Chapter 1 of this book takes the reader from the very south of the county and along the Wye Valley, taking in the county town of Hereford. The River Wye rises in the Plynlimon mountains east of Aberystwyth, near the spot where the Severn also has its source. The Wye enters England by Hay-on-Wye and winds its way through some of the most delightful scenery in the whole land, changing mood and direction from time to time and finally joining its original neighbour at the Severn Estuary. The whole of its length offers great touring and walking country, and the **Wye Valley Walk**, waymarked with the logo of the leaping salmon, follows the river closely for 112 miles, almost half of which are in Herefordshire. The valley was designated an Area of Outstanding Natural Beauty (AONB) in 1971, and the river itself was the first to be recognised as a Site of Special Scientific Interest (SSSI). The salmon logo is, of course, wholly appropriate, as the Wye is a mecca for anglers, with salmon the king of a realm that also includes perch, pike, tench, roach and eels. In the 18th cenruty artists, poets and the leisured classes enjoyed the Wye Tour, a highly agreeable alternative to the European Grand Tour, and two centuries later the car, train and bicycle have brought the charm of the valley within the reach of all.

SYMONDS YAT
MAP 1 REF E13
5 miles NE of Monmouth off the A40 and B4164

Travelling upstream, a journey through the southern part of the county starts at the beauty spot of Symonds Yat, an inland resort to which visitors flock to enjoy the views, the walks, the river cruises, the wildlife (peregrine falcons nest at Coldwell Rocks), the history and the adventure. Into the last category fall canoeing - rushing down the Wye gorge south of the village - and rock climbing. Symonds Yat (yat means pass) is divided into east and west by the Wye, with no vehicular bridge at that point. Pedestrians can make use of the punt ferry, pulled

Symonds Yat Chain Ferry

across the river by chain, but the journey by car is 4 ½ miles. Walking in the area is an endless delight, and at **The Biblins** a swaying suspension bridge provides vertiginous thrills across the river. Notable landmarks include the **Seven Sisters Rocks**, a collection of oolitic limestone crags; **Merlin's Cave**; King Arthur's Cave, where the bones of mammoths and other prehistoric creatures have been found; **Coldwell Rocks** and **Yat Rock** itself, rising to 500' above sea level at a point where the river performs a long and majestic loop. Also on the Symonds Yat walkabout is a massive boulder measuring 60' by 40', one of the largest in the country.

Walkers, birdwatchers and other lovers of the countryside find a peaceful, relaxed stopping place in Mike and Marion Servini's **Walnut Tree Cottage Hotel**. Located on the side of a picturesque valley, it overlooks the beautiful River Wye, and its large garden, with a walnut tree and three fish ponds, reaches down to a wood. Outside the two mid-19th century cottages that make up the hotel hanging baskets and flower tubs make a colourful sight in the summer, and inside, the scene is traditional, with exposed stone walls, original oils, beams and a wood-burning fire; the conservatory enjoys splendid views over the river.

Walnut Tree Cottage Hotel, Symonds Yat West, Near Ross-on-Wye, Herefordshire HR9 6BN Tel: 01600 890828

Five tastefully decorated bedrooms, all en suite, provide warm, comfortable and characterful overnight accommodation, and there are plenty of books and games to keep everyone happy. Excellent Italian-based cooking satisfies the hunger brought on by a day in the fresh air. Birdwatchers come to the area particularly to see peregrine falcons, who find the valley an ideal habitat and breeding ground.

Other entertainment in the area is provided by the **Jubilee Maze**, an amazing hedge puzzle devised by brothers Lindsay and Edward Heyes to celebrate Queen Elizabeth's 1977 Jubilee. On the same site is a museum of mazes and a puzzle shop (Tel: 01600 890630). In the **Jubilee Park**, at Symonds Yat West, is **The Splendour of the Orient** (Tel: 01600 890668), with Oriental water gardens, Chinese furniture, gifts from the Orient and a tea room and restaurant. Another major attraction in the Park is a garden centre with an extensive range of plants plus garden furniture and a gift

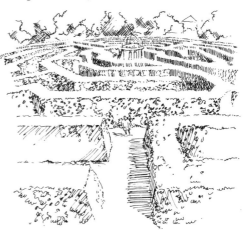

Jubilee Maze

shop. The church in Symonds Yat, built in the 14th century, is dedicated to St Dubricius, a local who converted the area to Christianity and who, according to legend, crowned King Arthur.

WHITCHURCH
4 miles NE of Monmouth off the A40

MAP 1 REF E13

Just north of Symonds Yat, in the shadow of the Rock, lies the village of Whitchurch, where at the **World of Butterflies** visitors can experience the warmth of a tropical hothouse with butterflies flitting freely about their heads. A little further up, and off, the A40, is **Kerne Bridge**, a settlement which grew around a bridge built in 1828, where coracles are still made, and from where the energetic walker can hike into history at the majestic **Goodrich Castle** in a commanding position above the Wye. Built of red sandstone in the 11th century by Godric Mapplestone, the castle is now ruined but still magnificent. It was the last bastion to fall in the Civil War, attacked by 'Roaring Meg', a siege gun cast in Whitchurch which could hurl a 200lb ball and which can now be seen in Hereford. The siege lasted four and a half months and marked the end of the castle's 'working life'. English Heritage maintain the ruins in excellent condition, and the 12th-century keep and elements from the next two centuries are well worth a visit, to walk the ramparts or just to imagine the glorious sight it once presented. Tel: 01600 890538

Torwood, near Whitchurch, is an interesting cottage garden by the village school, specialising in shrubs, conifers and herbaceous plants. Private visits welcome. Tel: 01600 890306

GOODRICH
6 miles NE of Monmouth off the A40

MAP 1 REF E13

Goodrich village is notable for the landmark 14th-century broach spire of its parish church. The vicar at a critical point in the Civil War was one Thomas Swift, grandfather of Jonathan Swift, author of *Gulliver's Travels*. This staunch Royalist hid some of the church's treasures, including a superb silver chalice, from the marauders, and, it is said, sewed 300 pieces of gold into his waistcoat to take to the King.

In a village of predominantly yellow sandstone houses, there are some notable Gothic exceptions; the most dramatic of these is **Ye Hostelrie Hotel**, whose pinnacles and tall lattice windows are a dramatic feature on the small village street. The core of the building dates from the 16th century and the present facade was added in 1850 - the work of Edward Blore, who had a hand in the design of Buckingham Palace. Inside, it's highly atmospheric, with exposed stone walls, a wealth of beams and an Elizabethan original among the fireplaces. Owners David and Heather Brown, who run the hotel with their son Matthew, are experienced hoteliers who offer a high level of service and hospitality "based on

Ye Hostelrie Hotel, Goodrich, Near Ross-on-Wye, Herefordshire HR9 6HX
Tel: 01600 890241

what we expect ourselves when travelling from home". The six individually decorated letting bedrooms all have en suite facilities, colour TV, clock-radio and courtesy tray. There are two restaurants, and all the food is home made and prepared to order, whether you choose from the bar menu, the à la carte list or the table d'hote. The carte ranges from Stilton paté and seafood ramekins to cod Mornay, grilled shark steak, duck breast with green peppercorn sauce and numerous ways with steak. Several vegetarian main courses are offered. Brown bread ice cream is one of the temptations on the dessert list. On the games front, the hotel has its own cricket team, two crib teams and two quiz teams. There's secure parking and a large cottage garden. The hotel overlooks the ruins of the castle.

ALONG THE RIVER MONMOW

A trip up from Monmouth along the the River Monmow, on and around the A466, will reward the motorist with not just beautiful scenery but a real glimpse into the often turbulent history of this Border country.

LLANROTHAL
MAP 1 REF D13
6 miles NW of Monmouth off the A466

Standing in isolation at the end of a lane by the river is the Church of St John the Baptist, built in the 12th and 13th centuries and restored from almost total ruin in the 1920s.

WELSH NEWTON
MAP 1 REF D13
4 miles N of Monmouth on the A466

The village lies right on the A466, and just off it stands **Pembridge Castle**, now in use as a private house. In the village churchyard of St Mary the Virgin lies the body of John Kemble, a Roman Catholic who was executed in 1679 for daring to hold a mass in the castle. A plain slab commemorates this martyr, who was 80 years of age when he met his violent end.

Several more castles along the River Monmow are further reminders that this pretty part of the world was once very turbulent.

SKENFRITH
MAP 1 REF D13
7 miles NW of Monmouth on the B4521

A drive or an energetic walk takes in the remains of **Skenfrith Castle** (the round tower is an impressive sight), an ancient mill and the Church of St Bridget, dating, like the castle, from the 12th and 13th centuries. And that's just in Skenfrith!

GROSMONT
MAP 1 REF C12
12 miles NW of Monmouth on the B4347

In the village of Grosmont lies another castle with impressive remains, and another interesting church, this one dedicated to St Nicolas of Myra.

A little way beyond Grosmont is **Kentchurch Court**, a one-time border castle rebuilt by John Nash around 1800 and featuring some splendid wood carvings by Grinling Gibbons. The Court has for many centuries been the home of the Scudamore family, one of whose number married Owen Glendower.

GARWAY
MAP 1 REF D12
9 miles N of Monmouth on a minor road

Marvellous views from the wild and remote **Garway Hill** take in the river valley, the Forest of Dean beyond Symonds Yat to the east, and the Black Mountains. The church at Garway was built by the Knights Templar and the influences from the Holy Sepulchre in Jerusalem can clearly be seen. During the purges of Henry VIII's reign, the Abbot of Monmouth was one of many who sought refuge in the church tower. The most unusual building in Garway is undoubtedly the famous

dovecote, the first of several to be mentioned in this book. A contemporary construction (also probably the work of the good knights) in a farmyard next to the church, the dovecote has precisely 666 pigeon-holes.

ROSS-ON-WYE
11 miles NE of Monmouth off the A40

MAP 1 REF E12

The lovely old market town of Ross-on-Wye is signalled from some way out by the towering spire of St Mary's Church, surrounded up on its sandstone cliffs by a cluster of attractive houses. Opposite the church is a row of Tudor almshouses which have an ancient yet ageless look and which show off the beauty of the rosy-red sandstone to great effect. The town was visited by the Black Death in 1637, and over 300 victims are buried in the churchyard. A simple stone cross commemorates these hapless souls, who were interred in the dead of night in an effort to avoid panicking the populace. Notable features in the church include 15th-century stained-glass figures and a tomb chest with effigies of William Rudhall, Attorney General to Henry VIII and founder of the almshouses, and his wife. Pride of place in the market square goes to the 17th-century **Market House**, with an open ground floor and pillars supporting the upper floor, which is a Heritage Centre. Spot the relief of Charles II on the east wall. The **Lost Street Museum** is a time capsule of shops and a pub dating from 1885 to 1935, while the **Button Museum** in Kyrle Street is unique in being the first museum devoted entirely to the humble - and sometimes not so humble - button, of which there are more than 8,000 examples on show spanning working clothes and uniforms, leisure pursuits and high fashion. A fascinating little place and a guaranteed hit with visitors - right on the button, in fact. Tel: 01989 566089.

Ross is full of interesting buildings, and besides those already noted is **Thrushes Nest**, once the home of Sir Frederick Burrows, a railway porter who rose above his station to become the last Governor of Bengal. Opposite Market House stands the half-timbered house (now shops) of the town's greatest benefactor, John Kyrle. A wealthy barrister who had studied law at the Middle Temple, Kyrle settled in Ross around 1660 and dedicated the rest of his life to philanthropic works: he donated the town's main public garden, **The Prospect**; he repaired St Mary's spire; he provided a constant supply of fresh water; and he paid for food and education for the poor. Alexander Pope was as impressed as anyone by this benefactor, penning these lines some time after the great man died in 1724 at the age of 87:

> *"Rise, honest Muse, and sing the Man of Ross,*
> *Health to the sick and solace to the swain,*
> *Whose causeway parts the vale in shady rows,*
> *Whose seats the weary traveller repose,*
> *Who taught that heav'n directed spire to rise?*
> *'The Man of Ross', each lisping babe replies."*

The **Ross International Festival** of music, opera, theatre, comedy and film takes place each August and grows in stature year by year. In and around Ross are several examples of modern public art, including leaping salmon metal sculptures (Edde Cross Street) and a mural celebrating the life of locally-born playwright Dennis Potter. At Ross-on-Wye Candlemakers in Gloucester Road (Tel: 01989 563697) are a shop and workshop showing the manufacture of all types of candles, with evening demonstrations and group visits by appointment.

In a quiet street running down to the River Wye, **Vaga House** is a tranquil hotel that attracts walkers, cyclists and tourists from all over the world. The hosts are Andy Campey, formerly a landscape gardener, and Jenny Gerred, who loves cooking and who will provide evening meals by arrangement. The house was built in 1780 by a boatman who plied his trade carrying cargo between Ross and Chepstow, and one of the original features to survive is a window in one of the bedrooms. These are seven in number, tastefully decorated in modern style, with everything needed for a warm, comfortable stay; two have en suite facili-

Vaga House, Wye Street, Ross-on-Wye, Herefordshire HR9 7BS
Tel: 01989 563024

ties. There are interesting photos of old Ross on the stairs, and superb views from the garden of a horseshoe bend in the river. At the front of the house hanging baskets and plant troughs produce a blaze of colour in summer. The owners have a dog and several cats, but guests are free to bring their own pets. Why Vaga? That was the Roman name for the Wye, meaning wanderer, and reflects the river's meandering course.

Jo Ashman, formerly a manager in the catering industry, changed direction when in June 1998 she opened **Halcyon Daze** on the historic market place. Her hobby and speciality is artistic craft products, and her shop attracts a wide cross-section of local people and tourists - in fact, anyone who appreciates well-designed and well-made ornamental pieces. Jo buys work from artists all

**Halcyon Daze, 6 Market Place, Ross-on-Wye, Herefordshire HR9 5NX
Tel: 01989 768719**

over the country and their output includes figures in glass, beautiful ceramic fish, steel dragons, medieval knights, and wizards of net and steel, dipped in resin and painted. There has been a building on the site since the early 1700s, and the shop was originally part of an arcade. The pristine premises allow the products to be displayed to best advantage, and visitors exploring the historic market town should definitely find time to look at the lovely pieces in Halcyon Daze. Open 9.30 to 5.30 except Sunday.

AROUND ROSS-ON-WYE

WILTON
MAP 1 REF E12

1 mile W of Ross on the A40

Wilton, just a short walk from Ross, stands at a crossing point of the River Wye. The bridge was built in 1599, some years after a river disaster which claimed 40 lives. Over the bridge are the ruins of **Wilton Castle**, of which some walls and towers still stand. An 18th-century sundial on the bridge bears this numinous inscription:

> *"Esteem thy precious time, which pass so swiftly away:*
> *Prepare them for eternity and do not make delay."*

Andrew Laskey's **Wilton Court Hotel** has the best of both worlds, combining a lovely quiet setting with easy access to and from the main road and motorway network. The hotel, built of red Forest of Dean stone in the 16th century, stands close to an old fording point on the River Wye, and its magnifi-

Wilton Court Hotel, Wilton, Near Ross-on-Wye, Herefordshire HR9 6AQ
Tel: 01989 562569

cent gardens have seats and tables set out on the river bank. A notable feature in the garden is a mulberry tree planted on behalf of King Charles to attract silk-worms and thus help to gratify his penchant for fine clothes. Wilton, now a suburb of Ross, was originally a port on the once totally navigable Wye; the hotel once served its court and was apparently linked by tunnel to the nearby jail. Beyond the original oak door are ancient panelling (also original) in the lounge bar, open fireplaces and some stained glass. The fireplace in the lounge is surmounted by an inset millstone. The 11 comfortably furnished bedrooms, all en suite, overlook gardens or the river. All are equipped with colour TVs, tea/coffee-makers, trouser presses and direct-dial phones. Guests can eat in the Old Bar areas or in the restaurant, which extends into a conservatory that looks out on to the gardens. Bar, à la carte and table d'hote menus provide abundant choice, using local supplies as much as possible, including Wye salmon and trout. Apple, celery and prawn salad is a popular starter, and among the main courses could be steak Romana (stuffed with Stilton and served with a port sauce) and chicken Wilton style with almonds and rosemary, flamed in brandy and dressed in a cream sauce. Children and pets may be accommodated by arrangement, but tranquillity is a valued commodity at this very special place.

WESTON-UNDER-PENYARD   Map 1 ref E12
2 miles E of Ross on the A40

Leave the A40 at Weston Cross to Bollitree Castle (a folly), then turn left to Rudhall and you'll come upon Kingstone Cottages, whose delightful informal gardens contain the National Collection of old pinks and carnations. Private visits welcome. Tel: 01989 656267

South of Weston lies **Hope Mansell Valley**, tucked away between the River Wye and the Forest of Dean, and certainly one of the loveliest and most fertile valleys in the region. It is an area of wooded hills and spectacular views, of farms and small settlements, with the tiny village of **Hope Mansell** itself at the far end. The **Forest of Dean**, over the border in Gloucestershire, is a vast and ancient woodland full of beauty and mystery, with signs of Iron Age settlement. Later a royal hunting ground, and the home of charcoal-burners and shepherds, it became the first National Forest Park.

ROSS-ON-WYE TO LEDBURY

YATTON   Map 1 ref E12
5 miles NE of Ross on the A449

In a remote farmyard setting off the B4224, Yatton Chapel, disused for many years, is a simple little church with a 12th-century doorway, a wooden belfry, agricultural floor and largely unplastered walls.

MUCH MARCLE
MAP 1 REF F11

7 miles NE of Ross on the A449

This is Big Apple Country, with major cider attractions in the shape of **Westons Cider Mill** (see below) and **Lyne Down Farm** (Tel: 01531 660691), where traditional methods of making cider and perry are still employed. In the church at Much Marcle is a rare painted wooden effigy, carved from solid oak and thought to be the likeness of a 14th-cenruty landowner called Walter de Helyon. Up until the 1970s he was painted a rather sombre stone colour, but was then loaned for an exhibition of Chaucer's London and was repainted in his original colours. The **Great Marcle Yew** is a talking point among all visitors to the village, its massive trunk hollowed out allowing up to eight people to enjoy cosy comfort on the bench inside.

A fascinating place to spend an hour or two is **Weston's Cider Mill**, the home of traditional Herefordshire cider-making for over a century. Situated just off the A449 midway between Ledbury and Junction 4 of the M50, it lies surrounded by cider-apple and perry-pear orchards in the wonderfully named village of Much Marcle. The business was founded by Henry Weston, a tenant farmer who took over The Bounds in the 1870s. Looking for a means of supplementing

**Weston's Cider Mill, The Bounds, Much Marcle, Near Ledbury,
Herefordshire HR8 2NQ Tel: 01531 660233**

his income from the farm, he made the decision to set up a commercial cider-making operation in 1880 which has grown steadily ever since. Fortunately, the original stone mill and screw press that were used in the early years have been retained, and they can now be seen in the beautiful grounds of the farmhouse. Still an independent family-owned business, Weston's is now an impressive cider-making operation which was the first of its kind in the country to receive the prestigious British Standard award for quality assurance.

Visitors can sample ciders with names like Stowford Press and Old Rosie, some of which are produced to recipes dating back well over a century. Tours of the cider mill lasting around two hours can be booked by writing or telephoning in advance; these incorporate a product tasting and take in the visitors centre and shop. At certain times, rides are also available on a wagon drawn by Weston's superb pair of Shire horses. Open Monday to Friday 9.30 to 4.30 and Saturday 10 to 1, all year round. While here, everyone should visit The Scrumpy House, a converted 17th century barn serving morning coffee, afternoon tea and daily home-cooked chef's specials: open Monday to Saturday 11 to 3, Sunday 12 to 3 and Friday & Saturday evenings 7 to 11 (booking recommended).

A short distance north of Much Marcle, **Hellens** (Tel: 01531 660668) is an untouched Tudor/Stuart house set in 15 acres of grounds with coppices, lawns and fishponds.

Closer to Ledbury, on the A4172 at **Little Marcle**, is **Newbridge Farm Park**, where families can enjoy a day out on the farm in the company of a large assortment of friendly farm animals. Tel: 01531 670780

LEDBURY

MAP 4 REF F11

10 miles NE of Ross on the A449

A classic market town filled with timber-framed black-and-white buildings, mentioned in the Domesday Book as Ledeberge and accorded its market status in the 12th century. The centre of the town is dominated by the **Barrett Browning Institute** of 1892, erected in memory of Elizabeth Barrett Browning, whose family lived at nearby Colwall. Alongside it are the almshouses of St Katherine's Hospital, founded in 1232 for wayfarers and the poor. **Church Lane**, much in demand for calendars and film location scenes, is a cobbled medieval street where some of the buildings seem almost to meet across the street. Here are the **Heritage Centre** in a timber-framed former grammar school (Tel: 01532 635680), **Butcher's Row Museum** (Tel: 01531 632040), and, upstairs in the old council offices, the **Painted Room**, graced with a series of remarkable 16th-century frescoes.

The town's symbol is the **Market House**, dating from about 1650 and attributed to John Abel, the royal carpenter, and another notable landmark is the Norman parish church of St Michael and All Angels, with a soaring spire set on a separate tower, some magnificent medieval brasses and bullet holes in the door - the scars of the Battle of Ledbury. The town's history has in general been

Market House, Ledbury

fairly placid, but its peace was broken with a vengeance in April 1645, when Royalist troops under Prince Rupert surprised a Roundhead advance from Gloucester. In the fierce fighting that followed there were many deaths, and 400 men were taken prisoner.

Annual events at Ledbury include a poetry festival in July, a street carnival in August and a hop fair in the autumn. Among the famous sons of the town is one of our most distinguished Poets Laureate, John Masefield. William Langland, who wrote *Piers Plowman,* was from nearby Colwall. The town is a great place for walking, and on the fringes nature-lovers will find plenty to delight in **Dog Hill Wood**, **Frith Wood** and **Conigree Wood**, as well as on **Wellington Heath** and along the **Old Railway Line**.

The lush Leadon Valley is the perfect centre for exploring the local country-side, and **Leadon House Hotel** is the perfect base. Tastefully refurbished in Edwardian style by owners Mike and Jan Williams, it has six spacious, compre-hensively equipped bedrooms, all with en suite bath or shower. Guests can relax in the comfortable lounge, enjoy a drink in the bar, or catch some sun in the conservatory or the Mediterranean-style courtyard. There's a choice of menus: the bar menu (last orders 8pm or by arrangement) and the main menu, which

Leadon House Hotel, Ross Road, Ledbury, Herefordshire HR8 2LP
Tel: 01531 631199

tempts with such dishes as tiger prawns with lime and chilli sauce, butterfly breast of chicken with Calvados and apple sauce, grilled swordfish, and mushroom stroganoff. Smoking is allowed only in the bar. Next to the hotel, the owners' Leadon Valley and Craft Centre offers an attractive range of antiques and a variety of quality craft gifts, many of them of local provenance. The hotel has a garden and courtyard.

2 ½ miles outside Ledbury on the A438 towards Tewkesbury stands **Eastnor Castle**, overlooking the Malvern Hills. This fairytale castle, surrounded by a deer park, arboretum and lake, has the look of a medieval fortress but was actually built between 1812 and 1824 and is a major example of the great Norman and Gothic architectural revival of the time. The first Earl Somers wanted a magnificent baronial castle, and, with the young and inspired architect Robert Smirke in charge, that's exactly what he got; the combination of inherited wealth and a judicious marriage enabled the Earl to build a family home to impress all his contemporaries. The interior is excitingly beautiful on a massive scale: a vast 60-feet high hall leads into a series of state rooms including a library in Italian Renaissance style containing a treasure house of paintings and tapestries, and a spectacular Gothic drawing room designed by Pugin. The grounds, part of which are a Site of Special Scientific Interest, are home to a wonderful variety of flora and fauna, and throughout the year the castle is the scene of special events. Tel:01531 633160

ROSS-ON-WYE TO HEREFORD

HOW CAPLE
MAP 1 REF E12
5 miles N of Ross on the B4224

The Edwardian gardens at **How Caple Court**, set high above the Wye in park and woodland, are magnificent indeed, with formal terraces, yew hedges, statues, pools, a sunken Florentine water garden and woodland walks. Tel: 01989 740626. How Caple's medieval **Church of St Andrew and St Mary** contains a priceless 16th-century German diptych depicting, among pther subjects, the martyrdom of St Clare and St Francis, and Mary Magdalene washing the feet of Christ.

BROCKHAMPTON
MAP 1 REF E12
6 miles N of Ross off the B4224

The **Church of All Saints** is one of only two thatched churches in the country and dates from 1902, designed by William Lethaby, who had close ties with Westminster Abbey, and built by Alice Foster as a memorial to her parents. The Norfolk thatch is not the only unusual aspect here, as the church also boasts stained glass made in the Christopher Whall studios and tapestries from the William Morris workshop from Burne-Jones designs. Continuing up the B4224 in the direction of Hereford, the visitor will come upon the village of **Fownhope**, where every year on Oak Apple Day in May or June the Green Man Inn celebrates the restoration of Charles ll with the Heart of Oak Club Walk. The inn's most famous landlord was Tom Spring, a champion bare-knuckle prize fighter who died in 1851. Fownhope church, 'The Little Cathedral', has a special treasure in the form of a tympanum of the Virgin and Child.

Minor roads lead eastward to another village not to be missed. **Woolhope** is named after Wuliva, Lady Godiva's sister, who owned the manor in the 11th century. In the 13th-century sandstone Church of St George is a modern stained-glass window depicting the siblings.

This is, like so much of the county, great walking country, with the **Marcle Ridge**, the 500' **Woolhope Dome** and the Forestry Commission's **Haugh Wood** among the attractions and challenges. The last is best approached from **Mordiford**, once a centre of the mining industry and now free from the baleful man-eating Mordiford Dragon. The story goes that the dragon was found by a local girl while it was still small. She nurtured it lovingly, and although it was at first content to feed on milk, and later chickens and the odd duck, it eventually developed a taste for cows and finally people. The beast terrorised the locals, and indeed one of the paths leading from the woods is still known as Serpents Lane. It was here that he would slink along the river to drink, and it is said that no grass ever grows there. No one was brave enough to face the beast until a man called Garson, who happened to be awaiting execution, decided that he had nothing to lose. He hid in a barrel by the river, and when the creature appeared he shot it through the heart. That was the end of the dragon, and also of poor Garson, who was killed in the fiery breath of the dragon's death throes. Mordiford stands on the River Lugg, just above the point where it joins the Wye, and the River Frome joins the Lugg a little way above the village. **Mordiford Bridge**, with its elegant span of nine arches, was once the source of regular revenue for the kings of this land: apparently every time the king crossed the bridge the locals lords had to provide him with a pair of silver spurs as a levy on the manor.

BRIDSTOW   MAP 1 REF E12
1 mile W of Ross off A49

St Bridget's Church enjoys a lovely, tranquil setting, like so many in the county. Dating from the 12th century, it was extensively restored in the 14th and 19th.

PETERSTOW   MAP 1 REF E12
2 miles W of Ross on A49

At **Broome Farm** (Tel: 01989 769556), half a mile off the A49, traditional farm-house cider has been brewed since the early 1980s, winning many prizes throughout the 90s and featuring apples with evocative names like Fox Whelp or Yarlington Mill. Also at Peterstow is **Kyrle House**, whose country garden contains herbaceous borders, a small grotto, sunken garden and secret garden. Private visits welcome. Tel: 01989 768412

MICHAELCHURCH   MAP 1 REF D12
5 miles W of Ross off the A4137

Another unpretentious church, hidden away down deep lanes in an idyllic setting by a pond. The Church of St Michael was built in the 11th or 12th century, with a Roman altar suggesting the earlier presence of a religious centre.

SELLACK   MAP 1 REF E12
3 miles NW of Ross on minor roads or off the A49

A popular waymarked walk takes in three marvellous churches in three delightful villages. The church in Sellack in uniquely dedicated to St Tysilio, son of a king of Powys, and is Norman in origin.

In a quiet village setting 2½ miles from the busy market town of Ross-on-Wye, Janet and Malcolm Hall's **Lough Pool Inn** is popular with anyone who likes good food! The three chefs use prime local ingredients to produce bar meals and a full menu with specialities that include beef in red wine with chestnuts, chicken ballotine and wild boar casserole. Wicked puds: cherries jubilee, white

**Lough Pool Inn, Sellack, Near Ross-on-Wye, Herefordshire HR9 6LX
Tel: 01989 730236**

chocolate bread pudding, hot chocolate fudge cake. The inn started life as 17th century cottages and was later a butcher's shop and a cider house. An old cider press stands in the large garden. The inn is also the start of the three-church walk that takes in Sellack, Kings Caple and Hoarwithy.

A short drive north of Sellack, in the churchyard at **King's Caple**, is a plague cross remembering victims of the Black Death of 1348. The church dates mainly from the 13th century and a fascinating little detail is to be found on the benefactors' board on the west wall. The local charities listed include Cake Money, a gift in perpetuity from a former vicar of King's Caple and Sellack. Pax cakes, signifying peace, are still distributed to the congregations on Palm Sunday.

HOARWITHY
MAP 1 REF E12
6 miles NW of Ross off the A49

By far the most extraordinary of the three walk-linked churches lies in the unspoilt village of Hoarwithy on the willow-lined banks of the Wye. **St Catherine's Church** is a splendid piece of architecture which owes its origin to the Reverend William Poole, who arrived in 1854, didn't like what he saw and spent the next 30 years supervising the building of a new church round the chapel. The result is an Italianate building complete with a campanile, arcades, beautiful tiled floors and a white marble altar with lapis lazuli inlay. Further on up or near the A49 are the villages of **Much Birch** and **Little Birch**, both with interesting churches. Also worth a look in Little Birch is **Higgin's Well**, named after a local farmer and restored at the time of Queen Victoria's Diamond Jubilee in 1897.

HOLME LACY   MAP 1 REF E11
5 miles SE of Hereford on the B4399

Holme Lacy was originally the estate of the de Lacy family in the 14th century, but later passed into the hands of the illustrious Scudamore family. The first Viscount Scudamore was the first person to classify the varieties of cider apple, and actually introduced the well-known Red Streak Pippin strain. The fine Palladian mansion dates from 1672 and once sported woodwork by Grinling Gibbons. St Cuthbert's Church, standing away from the village on a bend of the Wye, has a remarkable collection of 16th and 17th-century monuments of the Scudamores, and also some fine furnishings and medieval stalls with misericords.

Near the village of Holme Lacy is **Dinedor Court**, a splendid 16th-century listed farmhouse with an impressive oak-panelled dining hall. English Heritage is responsible for **Rotherwas Chapel** in **Dinedor**. This is a Roman Catholic chapel dating from the 14th and 16th centuries and featuring an interesting mid-Victorian side chapel and high altar.

HEREFORD

The county town-to-be was founded as a settlement near the unstable Welsh Marches after the Saxons had crossed the Severn in the 7th century. A royal demesne in the 11th century, it had a provincial mint, and was an important centre of the wool trade in the Middle Ages. Fragments of Saxon and medieval walls can still be seen, but the city's crowning glory is the magnificent *'Cathedral of the Marches'*. Largely Norman, it also has examples of Gothic, Early English, Decorated, Perpendicular and Modern architecture. The Cathedral demands an extended visit, as it contains, in the impressive New Library building, two of the country's most important historical treasures. *Mappa Mundi* is the renowned medieval world map, the work of Richard of Haldingham. Drawn on vellum, it has Jerusalem as its centre and East at the top, indicating that direction as the source of all things good and religiously significant. Richard was Treasurer of Lincoln Cathedral, which

Public Art in Hereford

might explain why Lincoln appears rather more prominently on the map than Hereford. The **Chained Library**, the finest in the land, houses 1500 rare books, including over 200 medieval manuscripts, all chained to their original 17th-century book presses. The Cathedral has many other treasures, including the shrine of St Thomas of Hereford in stone and marble, the Norman font, the Bishop's Throne and the John Piper tapestries. There's also a brass-rubbing centre. For details of the Cathedral's opening hours and guided tours call 01432 359880.

The Chained Library, Hereford

Hereford is full of fascinating buildings and museums which visitors should try to include in their tour. **Hereford Museum and Art Gallery** (Tel: 01432 260692) has a changing art gallery programme and hands-on exhibitions. The **Old Hall Museum**, right in the centre of High Town, brings alive the 17th century in a three-storey black-and-white house filled with fascinating exhibits. **Churchill House Museum** (Tel: 01432 267409), whose grounds include a fragrant garden, displays furniture, costumes and paintings from the 18th and 19th centuries; among its rooms are a costume exhibition gallery and Victorian nursery, parlour, kitchen and butler's pantry. The **Hatton Gallery** shows the work of local artist Brian Hatton. **St John Medieval Museum** at Coningsby (Tel: 01432 272837) is a 13th-century building in an ancient quadrangle of almshouses. Displays include costume models of Nell Gwynne, a famous daughter of Hereford, and the history of the Ancient Order of St John and its wars during the Crusades. Hereford's restored pumping station is home to the **Waterworks Museum** (Tel: 01432 361147), where Victorian technology is alive and well in the shape of a collection of pumps (some of which can be operated by visitors), a Lancashire Boiler and Britain's largest triple expansion engine. The **Regimental Museum** (Tel: 01432 359917) houses an important collection of uniforms, colours, medals, equipment, documents and photographs - and the flag and pennant of Admiral Doenitz.

Hereford and cider are old friends, and the **Cider Museum** (Tel: 01432 354207) tells the intersting story of cider production down the years. One of the galleries houses the King Offa distillery, the first cider brandy distillery to be granted a licence for over 200 years. Also on the outskirts of the city are the **Cider Mills** of HP Bulmer (Tel: 01432 352000), the world's leading cider producer. Look, learn and taste on one of the organised tours.

The original Saxon part of the city includes historic Church Street, full of 17th-century listed buildings (mostly modernised in the 19th century). Church Street and Capuchin Yard - the name derives from the hood worn by the Franciscan friars who built a chapel nearby - are renowned for their small specialist shops and craft workshops.

One of the most delightful places in the historic and thriving city of Hereford, **Nutters** is a wholefood coffee shop and licensed pavement café tucked away in a pretty little courtyard. The setting is an oasis of peace and calm in the middle of the city, decked with flower tubs from early spring; the tables set outside are ideal for a snack. Nutters offers morning coffee and afternoon tea, but for the full continental café effect, lunch in the sun with a glass of wine sees this charming place at its best. Owner Ken Mais, skilled photographer and collector of vintage bicycles, puts his culinary expertise to good use in producing wholesome vegetarian food using the best fresh produce. There is always a selection of excellent home-made cakes, plus teas, coffees, fruit juices, milkshakes, wine, ales and cider. Large-print and braille menus are available. No smoking inside. Open 9-6 daily except Sundays.

**Nutters, Capuchin Yard, off Church Street, Hereford,
Herefordshire HR1 2LT Tel: 01432 277447**

Hereford stages important musical events throughout the year, and every third year hosts the **Three Choirs Festival**, Europe's oldest music festival. The next one will take place in the Cathedral in August 2000.

HEREFORD TO HAY-ON-WYE
(via the Golden Valley)

KILPECK   MAP 1 REF D12
8 miles SW of Hereford off the A464

The parish **church of St Mary and St David** is one of the most fascinating in the whole county. Built by Hugh de Kilpeck (son of William Fitznorman, who built Kilpeck Castle) round an earlier Saxon church, it has changed little since the 12th century. Much of the church is unique in its rich decoration, but the gem is the portal over the south doorway, with all manner of elaborate carvings. Most of the carvings throughout the church have no apparent religioius significance, with some bordering on the bizarre, if not downright bawdy! Very little remains of the castle, it having been largely demolished by Cromwell's men, but on a clear day the castle mound affords very fine views.

Tourists who leave the main Hereford-Abergavenny road to see the fascinating Norman church in Kilpeck should stay a while longer to experience the delights of **The Red Lion Inn**. Both church and pub are just a mile from the main road. Besides the motorists, the customers include local farmers as well as holidaying walkers and cyclists, and in the winter two local shoots meet here.

The Red Lion, Kilpeck, Herefordshire HR2 9DN
Tel: 01981 570464

Angie and Rick Lovett are the friendly, welcoming hosts, and their long-haired German shepherd also wags a greeting. Brick-built, and topped by a slate roof, the pub is adorned by a particularly colourful display of hanging baskets, while inside are beamed ceilings and pictures showing the history of the village. A super pub garden overlooks the countryside. The food is home-cooked and mainly traditional, with barbecues in summer and well-kept ales, local cider and house wines. Children are very welcome. On the sporting side, the pub fields a darts team and two pool teams.

EWYAS HAROLD
Map 1 ref C12

12 miles SW of Hereford on the B4347

A village at the foot of the lovely Golden Valley, in an area of fine walks. West of the village lay the ancient Welsh kingdom of Ewias; the motte and bailey castle that was part of the border defences has disappeared, leaving only the distinctive mound.

Set in the centre of the village of Ewyas Harold on the edge of the Golden Valley of Herefordshire is the venerable **Temple Bar Inn & Restaurant**. Built in the 17th century, its character still remains, with open fires, stone walls and flagstone flooring in the atmospheric public bar. There are many stories as to

The Temple Bar Inn & Restaurant, Ewyas Harold, Herefordshire HR2 0EU
Tel: 01981 240423

how The Temple Bar acquired its name, one being that the inn was used as a court in the 18ᵗʰ and 19ᵗʰ centuries, when circuit judges would visit to hold court: thus it was named after Temple Bar in London, where the Inns of Court are to be found and where barristers sit their bar exams (the bar being the partition across a law court separating the judge and jury from the public. This popular public house is owned and run by husband-and-wife team Clark and Lorraine Castle and their keen and professional staff, with the additional ghost or two. The free house offers a warm and friendly atmosphere with home-cooked food, bar meals, an à la carte restaurant menu, Sunday lunches, children's menu and takeaway meals seven days a week. The pub provides a non-smoking restaurant and regular entertainment, with music, darts, pool, quoits and family quiz nights. In May of each year (the Spring Bank Holiday) The Temple Bar Inn hosts its now famed three-day beer festival in the Stable Bar, offering real ales from the most popular to the most unusual and live music for the duration of the festival. The inn is also the starting point for many fine walks and cycle trails through the Golden Valley. The quality and comprehensive facilities combined with the tranquil yet easily accessible location make The Temple Bar Inn one of the most pleasant stops in the beautiful Golden Valley.

ABBEY DORE   Map 1 ref C12
12 miles SW of Hereford on the B4347

A Cistercian **abbey** was founded here in the 12th century and the building, which was substantially restored by John Abel in the 17th century, is still in use as a parish church.

Dore Abbey

The garden at **Abbey Dore Court**, where the River Dore flows through the grounds, is home to many unusual shrubs and perennials, with specialist collections of euphorbias, hellebores and peonies. There's also a small nursery, a gift shop and a restaurant. Tel: 01981 420419.

The Neville Arms is a spacious country pub with bags of character, standing on the edge of the quiet village of Abbey Dore, a few miles north of the main Hereford-Abergavenny road (A465). Nuala Campbell, her

The Neville Arms, Abbey Dore, Herefordshire HR2 0AA
Tel: 01981 240319

partner Pete and her two sons provide a smiling welcome to a wide variety of regulars and casual visitors, including walkers, cyclists and motorists discovering the delights of the Golden Valley. The atmosphere inside is friendly and lively, and the pub is host to a darts ream and two pool teams. Overnight accommodation is provided in two en suite bedrooms, and there are facilities for disabled guests. The pub has a large car park, and a field where up to ten touring caravans may spend the night. Home-cooked food includes a traditional Sunday lunch. Abbey Dore has two other major attractions: the parish church built from the ruins of a Cistercian Abbey, and the marvellous garden at Dore Court oppsite the church. Another has recently been added in the form of llama trekking, the bookings for which are handled by the pub.

At nearby **Bacton**, a mile along the same B4347, is **Pentwyn Cottage Garden** (Tel: 01981 240508), where visitors can walk round the peaceful garden before enjoying a cream tea. From the remote, lonely roads that lead west towards Offa's Dyke and the boundary with Wales, motorists should leave their cars, stretch their legs and drink in the wonderful scenery. The villages of **Longtown** and **Clodock** lie at the foot of the **Olchon Valley**, while further north are the **Olchon Waterfall**, **Black Hill**, the rocky ridge of the **Cat's Back** and the ruins of **Craswall Priory**, which was founded in the 13th century by the rare Grandmontine order and abandoned 200 years later.

Back in the Golden Valley are the twin towns of **Turnastone** and **Vowchurch**, linked by a stone bridge over the river. These neighbours each have their own parish church.

PETERCHURCH

MAP 1 REF C11

10 miles W of Hereford on the B4348

The chief village of the **Golden Valley**, with a very fine parish church. In 786, King Offa brought monks to the village to found the original church. It was a sign of Offa's great power and influence that a bishop from Rome was included in the missionary party established here.

In the self-styled capital of the Golden Valley, surrounded by beautiful countryside, **Food for Thought** is a magnet for anyone who cares about good food. Robin Fair took over long-empty brick-built shop premises early in 1998 and converted them with great style and taste into a charming and civilised bistro-restaurant with a quarry-tiled floor and subdued lighting. Robin learned his culinary skills in London and Heidelberg, and uses the best and freshest of local produce for an imaginative, regularly changing menu that draws its inspiration from all parts of the world. All his dishes are cooked to order, and the fine food

Food for Thought, High Street, Peterchurch, Herefordshire HR2 0RP
Tel: 01981 550180

is accompanied by organic wines and beers. Booking is advisable, and smokers must refrain from lighting up until 10pm. Food for Thought is open Thursday-Sunday lunchtime and Tuesday-Saturday evening.

DORSTONE
MAP 1 REF C11

12 miles W of Hereford off the B4348

A very attractive village with neat sandstone cottages set around the green. St Faith's Church has a connection with Canterbury, as Richard de Brito, one of the knights who murdered Thomas à Becket, established a church here after serving 15 years' penance in the Holy Land for his crime. He returned to build the church and is buried in the churchyard.

South of Dorstone lie the ruins of **Snodhill Castle**, from which the views are spectacular even for this part of the world. To the north, on wild, exposed Merbach Hill, is the much-visited landmark of **Arthur's Stone**, a megalithic tomb of great antiquity which was used for the burial of tribal chieftains. Some say (but few believe it!) that the body of King Arthur himself was buried here.

From here the journey to Hay-on-Wye, a delightful border-straddling town, is but a short one.

HEREFORD TO HAY-ON-WYE
(along the Wye Valley)

The A465 out of Hereford soon reaches **Belmont Abbey**, whose architect, the renowned Pugin, was responsible for part of the House of Commons. One of the stained-glass windows in the church at **Clehonger** is probably also his work. The church at **Eaton Bishop**, just north fo the B4352, is famous for its east window, with 14th-century stained glass depicting the Crucifixion, Madonna and Child, and the Archangel Gabriel.

SWAINSHILL
MAP 1 REF D11

3 miles W of Hereford on the A438

The Weir in Swainshill is a charming riverside garden, spectacular in early spring, with 'drifts of flowering bulbs'. Views of the Wye and the Welsh Hills. National Trust. Tel: 01684 850051.

Partners David Young and Kevin Shaw, in the licensed trade all their working lives, are the affable hosts at **The Kites Nest Inn**, a peaceful spot in a stretched-out village on the busy A438 Hereford-Brecon road. On the Black & White Trail and the Wye Valley Walk, it attracts tourists and lovers of the great outdoors as well as a regular local clientele. The building is 18th century and in its 46-cover restaurant - originally a cider mill - the old beams are still in place, along with brasses, bottles, old cartwheels and lots of pictures. Home-cooked

**The Kites Nest Inn, Swainshill, Herefordshire HR4 7QA
Tel: 01981 590217**

meals, using local produce as much as possible, are served lunchtime and evening, and the menu changes daily. The pub has its own boules club and team and two pool teams, and in the Farmers Bar they play crib, dominoes and table skittles. Outside are hanging baskets, a flower garden and a play area with swings and a slide.

At **Credenhill**, a little way north of Swainshill on the A480, the **National Snail Farming Centre** is a unique attraction showing snail farming and a display of wild British snails both static and alive. Tel: 01432 760218

Further along the same road, seven miles from Hereford, is the village of **Yazor**, whose church, dating from the mid-19th century, features good stained glass and monuments, as well as a very colourful sanctuary.

MADLEY
MAP 1 REF C11
6 miles W of Hereford on the B4352

There's more fine stained glass in the church at Madley, where the immense stone font also takes the eye. St Dyfrig, the man who some say crowned King Arthur, was born here.

In the ancient village, just down the road from the famous church, **Marston Exotics** is home to one of the most exciting groups of plants in the world - the Insectivorous plants. This working nursery, the biggest in the country for its speciality, is run by Paul and Jackie Gardner, who offer an impressive variety of

Marston Exotics, Brampton Lane, Madley, Herefordshire HR2 9LX
Tel: 01981 251140 Fax: 01981 251649

these fascinating plants, and who can provide all the necessary advice and encouragement to beginners. Browsers can look at, and buy, anything from seedlings to mature 10-year-old plants, singly or in collections, and in addition to the insectivores, the nursery has a large retail area selling shrubs and heathers and trees. It is also home to the Natural Council for the Conservation of Plants & Gardens National Collection of Sarracenia, with more than 65 varieties and species. There's a café with a picnic area and homemade produce and crafts. The nursery has a busy mail order business, and the owners regularly exhibit at the major shows, including Chelsea, where they are winners of a Gold Medal. Open 8.30-4.30 Monday to Friday all year, also 1-5 Saturday and Sunday from March to October.

MOCCAS
10 miles W of Hereford off the B4352

MAP 1 REF C11

Moccas Court, designed by Adam and built by Keck, stands in seven acres of Capability Brown parkland on the south bank of the Wye. Tel: 01981 500381 for group bookings. In the village itself stands the beautiful Church of St Michael, built of the local stone known as tufa.

MONNINGTON-ON-WYE
10 miles W of Hereford off the A438

MAP 1 REF C11

The grounds of **Monnington Court**, part of the Bulmer Estate, cover 20 acres and include a lake, river, sculpture garden, a famous mile-long avenue of firs and yews, and the foundation farm of the British Morgan horse. There's also a cider mill. Private visits by appointment. Tel: 01981 500698.

KINGSTONE   Map 1 ref D11
7 miles SW of Hereford on the B4348

Webton Court is a black and white Georgian farmhouse. It is a 200-acre working farm set in the heart of the Wye Valley specialising in livestock and cider fruit. A good base for touring, it is only seven miles from the ancient city of Hereford. Hay-on-Wye, famous for its bookshops, and the Black and White vil-

Robert and Gill Andrews, Webton Court Farmhouse, Kingstone, Near Hereford, Herefordshire HR2 9NF Tel: 01981 250220

lages of Weobley, Pembridge and Eardisland are all within 20 miles. The accommodation consists of spacious bedrooms with wash basin, tea and coffee facilities and colour TV. There are two ground-floor en suite rooms suitable for disabled guests. Evening meals are served by prior arrangement and locally produced meat and vegetables are always used when available.

HAY-ON-WYE   Map 1 ref B11
18 miles W of Hereford on the B4348

And so to the border town of Hay-on-Wye, where bookworms will wriggle with delight as they browse through its 38 secondhand bookshops. Richard Booth, known as the King of Wye, opened the first bookshop here 40 years ago, and is a leading player in the annual **Hay Book Festival**. The famous diarist Francis Kilvert was a local man, and his Diary is just one of millions of books on for sale.

But books are not the only attraction: Hay also has a large number of antique shops, and as we have seen more or less throughout this opening chapter, the River Wye in never far away, with its shifting moods and ever-changing scenery.

2 North Herefordshire

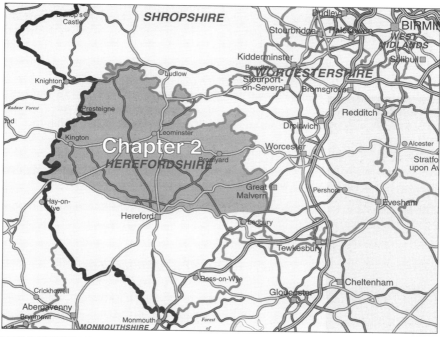

Back to Hereford for the start of a trip through the northern part of the county, including the towns of Bromyard, Leominster and Kington, and the wonderful Black and White villages that are among the most picturesque in the whole of England.

HEREFORD TO BROMYARD

SUTTON ST NICHOLAS
MAP 1 REF E11

4 miles NE of Hereford off the A465

Just outside the village is a group of stones known collectively as the **Wergin Stone**. In the hollow base of one of the stones, rents or tithes were laid, to be collected later by the local squire. There is a story that in 1652 the Devil picked up the stone and removed it to a spot a little distance away. It took a team of nine oxen to return the stone to its original place, though why the villagers bothered is not related. South of the village is the Iron Age hill fort of **Sutton Walls**, where King Offa once had a palace. One day in 794, Offa, the King of Mercia, promised the hand of his daughter Alfreda to Ethelbert, King of East Anglia. Ethelbert journeyed to Sutton Walls, but the trip was full of bad omens: the earth shook, there was an eclipse of the sun, and he had a vision that his mother was weeping bloody tears. In spite of all this he pressed on, but after he had reached the palace, and before the wedding ceremony, Offa had him beheaded. There is little now to see at the camp, as a lot of the land has been worked on. Many skeletons have been unearthed, some showing signs of very violent ends.

Just outside Sutton, **Overcourt Garden Nursery** is situated in the grounds of a Grade ll listed 16th-century house with connections to the Crusader Knights of St John. A wide range of unusual plants is for sale. Private visits welcome. Tel: 01432 880845.

MUCH COWARNE   MAP 1 REF E10
8 miles NE of Hereford off the A465

The Fir Tree Inn is one of this book's most versatile establishments, dealing not only in food and drink but also offering seasonal accommodation in static holiday caravans and fishing on a quiet lake in the four acres of grounds. The inn, built in the 16th century and later extended and sympathetically modernised, has very experienced owners in Richard and Lynne Swain, both in the business all their working lives. Richard is a highly trained and very talented chef, and a meal in the Hereford Restaurant is always a treat to look forward to. The choice is very extensive and includes both English classics and dishes with a touch of the exotic. The Worcester Room offers great bar meals, and in the Ledbury Bar the locals enjoy a game of pool, darts or dominoes. The Malvern Suite is a

The Fir Tree Inn, Much Cowarne, Herefordshire HR7 4JN
Tel: 01531 640619

popular venue for social occasions and conferences. In the garden, the 'magic tree house', with its swing and slide, keeps young visitors happy for hours.

MORETON JEFFRIES
MAP 1 REF E10

8 miles NE of Hereford off the A465

Worth a visit here is a long, low church with a little slatted bell tower. Note the elaborately carved Jacobean puplit, complete with sounding board and reading desk - a sophisticated touch in generally simple surroundings.

PENCOMBE
MAP 1 REF E10

10 miles NE of Hereford off the A465

The **Shortwood Working Dairy Farm** (Tel: 01885 400205) is home to miniature ponies, giant shire horses, cattle, pigs and hens.

BROMYARD
MAP 1 REF F10

13 miles NE of Hereford on the A44

A super little market town on the River Frome, with hills and good walking all around. In the town itself the **Teddy Bear Museum** (Tel: 01885 488329), housed

in an old bakery, is a magical little world of bears, dolls and Disney-related toys. It also has a bear hospital.

Bromyard Heritage Centre (Tel: 01885 482038) tells the stories of the local hop-growing industry, the railway age and life in Bromyard through the centuries. Find time to look at the 12th-century St Peter's Church with its historic Walker organ. Late June and early July see Bromyard's **Great Hereford Show and Steam Rally**, an event which has been built up to major proportions over the years. Later on, in early September, **Bromyard's Folk Festival** brings in the crowds.

Teddy Bear Museum, Bromyard

Brian Gibbons and his staff have turned **The Crown & Sceptre** into the town's most popular hostelry, with a strong following among both locals and visitors to Bromyard. It stands in the centre of town opposite the Teddy Bear Museum, and the final stage of its renovation was the creation of a covered entrance from the car park. The original deeds show the Grade ll listed building to be over 350 years old, a fact evidenced by the splendid beams and stonework. Booking is advisable in the 24-cover restaurant, where a full selection of meat,

The Crown & Sceptre, Sherford Street, Bromyard, Herefordshire HR7 4DL
Tel: 01885 482441

fish and vegetarian dishes is served, along with traditional puddings. There's also a good menu of bar snacks. For guests wishing to stay overnight the pub offers five cosy bedrooms, all en suite, one of them with a four-poster bed.

In the same ownership as the Wye Valley Brewery in Hereford, **The Rose & Lion** is a thoroughly likeable drinking pub where regulars and outsiders down a glass or two over conversation in a delightfully old-world atmosphere. The old tap room, recently refurbished and flagstone-floored, is a perfect spot for quenching a thirst, and at the back there's an equally appealing beer garden. The building dates from 1823 and has carried its present name since 1851, when it began brewing its own beer. That no longer happens, but quality ales on tap include

The Rose & Lion, 5 New Road, Bromyard, Herefordshire HR7 4AJ
Tel: 01885 482381

Wye Valley Bitter and HPA, Butty Bach (a Beer of the Year award-winner at the Cardiff Beer Festival) and always something from the Dorothy Goodbody range. Fran Herdman is the tenant, running this charming 'wet' pub with the help of her son Andrew and daughter Pip.

AROUND BROMYARD

BROMYARD DOWNS
MAP 1 REF F10
1 mile NE of Bromyard off the B4203

A walk on the beautiful Bromyard Downs will set you up perfectly for a visit to **The Royal Oak**, a fine old pub with a history reaching back more than 300 years. It's very much a family affair, offering a smiling welcome and personal service: Mick and Angie run the show, with son Richard in the kitchen. The pub, which lies a mile north of the A44 east of Bromyard, has a beamed lounge bar with log fire, flagstone floor, old prints and Angie's growing collection of ornamental pigs; a games bar; and a cosy restaurant with fabulous views across to the Welsh Black Mountains. The same view is enjoyed by the function room, which can accommodate 100 for a sit-down meal. Richard's repertoire spans special salads (a summer favourite), fish and meat main courses, a good vegetarian selection and tempting home-made puddings. There are children's menus and 'small bite' meals. Booking is recommended for dinner at weekends and the Sunday lunch carvery. Real ales, local cider, good house wines. Around the pub

The Royal Oak, Bromyard Downs, Bromyard, Herefordshire HR7 4QP
Tel: 01885 482585

are pleasant gardens created by Angie and cared for by her father Bert, a wooded area that's perfect for children to have fun, and a popular parking spot for caravans. The owners have seven Staffordshire bull terriers, but they welcome visitors' dogs - and even provide towels for wet shaggy dogs!

STANFORD BISHOP

MAP 1 REF F10

2 miles E of Bromyard off the B4220

Great walking is to be enjoyed on rugged **Bringsty Common**, and for the energetic the walk can take in the National Trust property of **Lower Brockhampton**, a 14th-century half-timbered moated farmhouse with a very unusual, tiny detached gatehouse. Springtime sees it at its best, when the daffodils provide a mass of colour. South of Bringsty Common, the church at Stanford Bishop has the very chair occupied by St Augustine at a 7th-century bishops' conference. The yew tree in the churchyard is the largest in the area.

On the B42202 among lovely rolling hills south of Bromyard, Reg and Sarah Orme's **Hereford House Inn** is a great place to stop for a drink and a meal. The extended 17th century house enjoys a most attractive setting, with fields next to the car park - where caravaners are welcome to spend the night - and a beer garden looking south to the Malvern Hills. Inside are two inviting rooms adorned with old plates and brasses, and scenes of the area painted by local artists. Good-

Herefordshire House Inn, Malvern Road, Stanford Bishop, Near Bromyard, Herefordshire WR6 5TT Tel: 01886 884252

value bar snacks and grills use prime fresh produce, and many dishes are accompanied by Sarah's super chips. The traditional Sunday roast is always very popular. The pub attracts a wide variety of visitors, including ramblers, cyclists, fishermen and hop-pickers, and the harvest festival is just one of the events organised by the owners for the benefit of local charities. Open all day in season, evenings only November to February.

EDVIN LOACH   MAP 1 REF F9
4 miles N of Bromyard off the B4203

Here are the remains of one of Britain's rare Saxon churches. The church at nearby Edwyn Ralph is noted for its unusual monument and medieval effigies under the tower.

HEREFORD TO LEOMINSTER

HOPE UNDER DINMORE   MAP 1 REF D10
8 miles N of Hereford on the A49

Queen's Wood Country Park is a popular place for walking and enjoying the panoramic views, and the most visited spot of all is the arboretum with its wonderful variety of specimen trees.

Adjoining the park is **Dinmore Manor and Gardens** (Tel: 01432 830410), where the Knights Hospitallers had their local headquarters. The gardens are sheltered, but as they rise some 550' above sea level, they afford marvellous views across to the Malvern Hills. The gardens are a sheer delight, and among the many attractions are a 12th-century chapel near the rock garden and pools, a cloister with a roof walk, wonderful stained glass, a yew tree believed to be 1,200 years old, medieval sundials and a grotto. Many varieties of plants, shrubs, alpines and herbs are available for sale in the Plant Centre.

LEOMINSTER   MAP 1 REF D9
13 miles N of Hereford on the A49

The hub of the farming community and the largest town in this part of the county, made wealthy in the Middle Ages through wool, and still prospering today. Leominster (pronounced Lemster) is well known as one of the most important antiques centres in the region. Some have linked the unusual name with Richard the Lionheart, but there was in fact an earlier king who earned the title. In the 7th century, Merewald, King of Mercia, was renowned for his bravery and ferocity and earned the nickname of 'the Lion'. He is said to have a dream concerning a message from a Christian missionary, while at the same time a religious hermit had a vision of a lion coming to him and eating from his hand. They later met up at what was to be Leominster almost by accident, and when the King heard of the hermit's strangely coincidental dream, he was persuaded to convert to Christianity. Later, the King requested that a convent and church be built in the town; a stone lintel on the west door of the church depicts the chance meeting of King and hermit. Other, more likely explanations of the name revolve around Welsh and medieval Latin words for 'stream' and 'marsh'.

The Priory **Church of St Peter and St Paul**, originally King Merewald's convent, became a monastery in the 11th century, and the three naves, built in the 12th, 13th and 14th centuries, attest to its importance. A curio here is a ducking stool which, in 1809, was the last to be used in England.

Leominster Priory Church

A short walk away, in Priory Park, is **Grange Court**, a fine timbered building which for many years stood in the market place. Built in 1633, it is the work of John Abel, and shows typical Abel flamboyance in its elaborate carvings.

Other buildings to be visited in Leominster are the **Leominster Folk Museum** (Tel: 01568 615186), the Lion Gallery (Tel: 01568 611898), featuring the best of local arts and crafts, and the Forbury, a 13th-century chapel dedicated to Thomas à Becket.

The busy market town of Leominster is a natural gathering place for the local farming community and also attracts visitors from around the world to its renowned antiques shops and markets. Locals and strangers both appreciate the

**The Chequers Inn, Etnam Street, Leominster, Herefordshire HR6 8AE
Tel: 01568 612473**

quiet, relaxed ambience of **The Chequers Inn**, where John and Val Richardson provide a smiling welcome, a regularly changing selection of real ales and an appealing, reasonably priced menu that caters for all tastes, including vegetarian. The building, of stone and oak under a slate roof, goes back to the 14th century. Outside, plant troughs and hanging baskets make a cheerful display, and a beer garden with a wishing well beckons in the summer months. The old-fashioned interior features an open fire, old beams, ornamental brass and several ancient firearms. In the lounge hang a pair of carriage lamps and two navigation lamps. There is a function room and a small restaurant. The pub fields male and female darts teams and a quiz team, and card games and indoor quoits are also played.

AROUND LEOMINSTER

STOKE PRIOR   MAP 1 REF D9
2 miles SE of Leominster off the A44

The Lamb is a really delightful old-world inn, a must for anyone visiting the tiny, picturesque village of Stoke Prior. Yvonne and Ron Painter are the tenants, helped by Yvonne's parents Margaret and Keith, and their hospitality is a key

**The Lamb Inn, Stoke Prior, Near Leominster, Herefordshire HR6 0NB
Tel: 01568 760308**

factor in the appeal of the inn. Food is served lunchtime and evening seven days a week, and in the traditional surroundings of the dining area all appetites are catered for on a menu that encompasses salads, baguette sandwiches, interesting starters (filo prawn parcels with lemon and dill sauce) and a long list of main courses. Desserts include a hard-to-resist golden syrup sponge pudding. A selection of real ales always features two hand-pumped guest ales, one of them brewed in the village. At the back of the inn there's a beer garden and an area where children can play in safety.

KIMBOLTON
MAP 1 REF D9
3 miles NE of Leominster off the A49

For anyone wanting a break in the country with tranquillity, picturesque scenery and good food, **Lower Bache House** is an ideal choice. Nestling in 14 acres of private nature reserve set in a tiny, unspoilt valley, a substantial 17th-century stone farmhouse has been lovingly restored by resident owners Rose and Leslie Wiles, who have retained the historical features and the wealth of oak beams while incorporating modern amenities. The old granary has been made into three delightful suites, each with its own sitting room and ensuite bath or shower room. Low beamed ceilings, half-timbered walls and period pine furniture impart a feeling of warmth and cosiness, and watercolours and 19th century maps and prints complete the picture. Another room in similar style is in the former stables across the courtyard. A meal in the atmospheric converted cider-making annexe is quite an event, whether it's breakfast with home-made sausages, free-range eggs and kippers and haddock from their own smokehouse, or a set dinner using as much as possible organic meat and produce, much of it from the kitchen

**Lower Bache House, Kimbolton, Near Leominster,
Herefordshire HR6 0EP Tel: 01568 750304**

garden. Typical delights could include smoked salmon mousse, poached gurnard, duck breast with a port and wild mushroom sauce, and crème brûlée with an orange and Grand Marnier compote. A terrace leading off the dining room enjoys lovely views of the valley. No children under 8. No pets. No smoking. ETB Highly Commended.

There are two delightful gardens to visit near Kimbolton. At **Stockton Bury** (turn right off the A49 on to the A4112) the sheltered four-acre garden has an extensive variety of plants set among medieval buildings, a kitchen garden, pigeon house, tithe barn, cider press and ruined chapel. At **Grantsfield** (turn right off the A49) are the gardens of an old farmhouse with a wide range of unusual plants and shrubs, old roses, climbers, orchard, kitchen garden - and superb views. Private visits welcome. Tel: 01568 613338.

KINGSLAND   MAP 1 REF D9
3 miles NW of Leominster off the A4110

Stuart and Alison Rees, Sue Jennings and Richard Dawes are partners in a superb village inn in a pretty village three miles northwest of Leominster. **The Corners Inn**, prominently situated and easy to spot with its immaculately whitewashed and timbered facade, dates back in part to the 16th century, and the back bar is particularly appealing with its low ceiling and gnarled beams. In contrast, the galleried dining area is light and spacious, with tables set neatly under great timbers in what was formerly a hay barn. Sue and Alison do the cooking and their menus are full of good things, from garlic and coriander mushrooms and

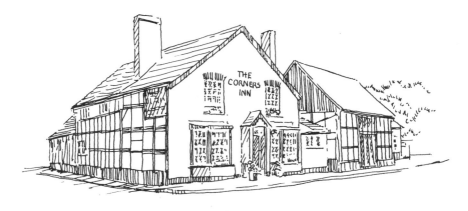

The Corners Inn, Kingsland, Near Leominster, Herefordshire HR6 9RY
Tel: 01568 708385 Fax: 01568 709033

deep-fried brie to steaks, spicy fried chicken and roast monkfish served with aioli on a bed of herb couscous. Food is served lunchtime and evening every day, and although there are seats for 100, the restaurant's popularity makes booking a must at weekends. Ring also for details of overnight accommodation, which was due to come on stream after we published.

ASHTON
MAP 1 REF D9

3 miles N of Leominster on the A49

Three miles north of Leominster on the road to Ludlow stands the National Trust's **Berrington Hall**, an elegant 18th-century mansion designed by Henry Holland (later architect to the Prince Regent) in parkland laid out by his father-in-law Capability Brown. Features of the interior include a spectacular staircase hall, gilt tracery, fine furniture and paintings, a nursery, Victorian laundry and tiled Georgian dairy. Most notable of all are perhaps the beautifully decorated ceilings: in the drawing room, the central medallion of Jupiter, Cupid and Venus is a composite scene taken from *The Council* and *The Banquet of the Gods* by Penni and del Colle in the Villa Farnesina in Rome. In the grounds are a walled garden with a collection of old-fashioned local apple trees, a woodland walk and a living willow tunnel in the children's play area. Tel: 01568 615721.

YARPOLE
MAP 1 REF D9

4 miles N of Leominster off the B4361

In this delightful village with its jumble of cottages and their colourful gardens stands the Church of St Leonard, which has a detached bell tower, a wooden structure with a stone outer wall. At neighbouring **Eye** are **Eye Manor** and the **Church of St Peter and St Paul**, where Thomas Harley, a Lord Mayor of London, is buried. An unusual feature of this church is the pulpit with carvings of Red Indians.

Near Yarpole, reached from the B4362 between Bircher and Mortimer's Cross, stands **Croft Castle**, an atmospheric property in the care of the National Trust. Behind a defensive exterior that tells of the troubled times of Marcher territory, the state rooms are elegant and comfortable, with rare furniture, fine plasterwork and portraits of the Croft family, who have occupied the place with only one break since it was built in the 14th century. In the park are ancient oaks and an avenue of 350-year-old Spanish chestnut trees. Tel: 01568 780246. Also looked after by the National Trust, and just a short walk away, is **Croft Ambrey**, an Iron Age fort which affords stunning views.

ORLETON
MAP 1 REF D9

6 miles N of Leominster off the B4361

The churchyard at Orleton is thought by some to be the likely setting for the Resurrection at the Day of Judgemnt, and for that reason people from all over the country used to ask to be buried here in the hope that they would be among the first in the queue when life began again. The road north from Orleton leads to **Richard's Castle** on the Shropshire border. This Norman castle, which lies in ruins on the hillside above the church, was, like so many others, built as a defence against the marauding Welsh. The church played a similar role, and in the 14th century it was refurbished for use as a chapel by the Knights Hospitallers.

MORTIMER'S CROSS
MAP 1 REF D9

7 miles NW of Leominster on the A4110/B4362

The site of one of England's greatest and bloodiest battles. Here, on 3 February 1461, was enacted the final episode in the War of the Roses, with the Yorkists defeating the Lancastrians. Hundreds died that day, but Edward Mortimer, the Duke of York's eldest son, survived and was crowned King Edward IV in the following month. Visit the Battle Centre at Watermill.

WIGMORE
MAP 1 REF C8

11 miles NW of Leominster on the A4110

A few miles on from Mortimer's Cross, Wigmore is noted for its ruined **castle** and abbey. With its impressive vantage point, the hillside at Wigmore was a natural site for building a castle, which is what William FitzOsbern did in the 11th century. This was one of a chain of fortifications built along the Welsh border. By the time of his death in 1071, FitzOsbern had also built Chepstow, Berkeley, Monmouth, Guenta (perhaps Winchester?) and Clifford, and had re-built Ewyas Harold. Wigmore passed into the hands of the Clifford family, then the ambitious Mortimers, and it was no doubt here that the future Edward IV prepared himself for the battle at Mortimer's Cross. Enough of the ruins remain to show that Wigmore was once a very serious castle, and one which protected the village and its environs for many centuries, until the Civil War. Two miles north of the village are signs to the 12th-century **Wigmore Abbey**, now in use as a private residence.

Ye Olde Oak Inn has been a pub for at least 100 years, but the narrow whitewashed building is more than 300 years old. It stands in the heart of Wigmore on what was formerly a busy drovers' road, and remains the hub of life in a village which once had its own court and prison and was home to more than 2,000 (the population now is around 400). Hands-on owners Roy and Dawn put a major emphasis on food, and bookings are needed at weekends for a table in either the quaint conservatory restaurant (no smoking) or in the lounge

Ye Olde Oak Inn, Wigmore, Herefordshire HR6 9UJ
Tel: 01568 770247

dining area for people who prefer to smoke. Roy is a classy chef and his menu spans a wide range of dishes, from sirloin and rump steaks (very popular and highly recommended), to chilli, spicy prawns in pitta bread and several mouth-watering ways with chicken. Bar snacks (burgers and jacket potatoes) are available every lunchtime except Sundays and Bank Holidays. This is a deservedly popular pub, with lots of repeat business, and it also offers accommodation - phone for details.

BRAMPTON BRYAN
MAP 1 REF C8
16 miles NW of Leominster on the A4113

Many of the thatched cottages in the village as well as its castle, had to be rebuilt after a siege during the Civil War in 1643. The chief relic of the castle is the gatehouse, which now stands in the gardens of a charming 18th-century house near the Church of St Barnabus. Sir Robert Harley, a relation of Thomas Harley of Berrington Hall, owned the castle, and it was due to his allegiance to Cromwell that it was besieged not once but twice by the Royalist army. Following the eventual destruction of the castle by the Royalists, Harley fell out with Cromwell. They remained at loggerheads until the day that Cromwell died, and on that day in September 1658 it is said that a violent storm swept through Brampton Bryan Park, destroying a great number of trees. Harley was convinced that the storm was the Devil dragging Cromwell down to Hell.

SHOBDON

MAP 1 REF C9

8 miles W of Leominster on the B4362

The **Church of St John the Evangelist**, which stands on the site of a 12th-century priory, is one of the most remarkable in the county. Behind a fairly unremarkable facade, the interior is stunning. The overall effect is of being in a giant wedding cake, with white and pale blue icing everywhere, and lovely stained glass adding to the dazzling scene.

Just north of here are the **'Shobdon Arches'**, a collection of Norman sculptures which have sadly been greatly damaged by centuries of exposure to the elements, but which still demonstrate the high skills of the sculptors of the 12th century.

In the unspoilt area known as The Marches, on the border with Wales, **The Paddock** is a long single-storey house purpose built for B&B in 1996. It's a great base for walkers, cyclists and anyone touring this area of outstanding natural

The Paddock, Shobdon, Near Leominster, Herefordshire HR6 9NQ
Tel: 01568 708176

beauty, and proprietors Sheila and Mick Womersley are always on hand to provide a friendly welcome. The five bedrooms are modern, spacious and spotlessly clean; all are en suite and have tea-makers, colour TV, hairdryers, clock-radios, ceiling fans and either iron and board or trouser press. Underfloor central heating can be individually controlled, and a mechanical ventilation system guarantees a constant supply of pollen-free air. The ground floor location is a particular boon for elderly or less mobile guests. The guest lounge, with comfortable settees, satellite TV, magazines and local information, is a good place for relaxing, while the large garden and patio beckon when the sun shines. A three-course dinner is served at 7 o'clock (bring your own wine) with a choice of starters and sweets around the two main-course options - perhaps beef braised in red wine or turkey fillet in an apricot and brandy sauce. No smoking. No pets. AA selected and ETB Highly Commended.

Country roads signposted from the B4362 lead west from Shobdon to **Lingen**, where the **Nursery and Garden** are a horticultural haven for visitors to this remote area of the Marches. The gardens are home to National Collections of Iris Sibirica and Herbaceous Campanula. Tel: 01544 267720.

Even nearer the Welsh border, between **Kinsham** and **Stapleton** (signs from the B4362 at **Combe**) is **Bryan's Ground**, a three-acre Edwardian garden with topiary, parterres, formal herb garden, shrubbery and apple orchard, plus a specialist collection of old roses. Tel: 01544 260001.

THE BLACK AND WHITE VILLAGE TRAIL
(a Round Trip)

The **Black and White Trail** was devised in 1987 by David Gorvett, who wanted to encourage visitors to take a leisurely look at some of the most beautiful countryside and the most picturesque villages in England. The trail can be used by motorists and cyclists, but best of all is to walk from village to village, each of them a treasury of cottages, inns and shops and each with a fascinating parish church.

MONKLAND   Map 1 ref D9
3 miles W on Leominster on the A44

The Monkland Arms, on the A44 west of Leominster, has found a new lease of life in the capable and enthusiastic hands of Margaret and Jeffrey Hill, who spent many months in a stylish renovation programme before re-opening its doors as the the new owners in 1996. A pub has stood on the site for 250 years, and previous names included the Red Lion and the Travellers Rest. Margaret and Jeffrey, through their application and personalities, have made it a very popular place for both local residents and tourists, and it is particularly busy at weekends. Margaret is a talented cook, and booking is recommended at week-

**The Monkland Arms, Monkland, Near Leominster,
Herefordshire HR6 9DE Tel: 01568 720259**

ends for a table in the restaurant. On the less formal bar menu jacket potatoes, burgers, fish dishes and steaks are the most popular orders. There were plans as we went to press (summer 1999) to make available a self-catering holiday flat with its own entrance - phone for the latest information.

STRETFORD   MAP 1 REF D10
4 miles SW of Leominster off the A4110

Stretford has a most unusual church that is almost as wide as it is long. Massive timber screens go across the church, dividing naves from chancels, with a Jacobean pulpit in the middle. The church is dedicated to St Cosmas and St Damian, patron saints of physicians and surgeons.

DILWYN   MAP 1 REF C10
7 miles W of Leominster on the A4112

The village lies in a hollow, so its Old English name of 'Secret Place' is an appropriate one. The main body of the parish church was built around 1200, with additions in the following century and a spire put up in the 18th. The workmen who built the church were also associated with nearby **Wormsley Priory**, and one of the figures in Dilwyn's church is thought to be a member of the Talbot family, founders of the priory. The church registers go back over 400 years, providing a valuable trail of local history.

WEOBLEY   Map 1 ref C10
9 miles SW of Leominster on the B4230

The steeple of the parish church of St Peter and St Paul is the second highest in the county, a reminder that this prettiest of places (call it Webbly) was once a thriving market town. One of its more unusual sources of wealth was a successful glove-making industry which flourished in the early 19th century when the Napoleonic Wars cut off the traditional French source of gloves. At certain times in its history Weobley returned two Members of Parliament, but there have been none since 1832. One of the effigies in the church is of Colonel John Birch, who was rewarded for his successes with Cromwell's army with the Governorship of Hereford and who later became a keen Royalist and Weobley's MP. Little but the earthworks remain of Weobley Castle, which was built before the Norman Conquest and was captured by King Stephen in 1138. One of Weobley's many interesting buildings is called **The Throne**, but it was called The Unicorn when King Charles l took refuge after the Battle of Naseby in 1645.

The delightful half-timbered village of Weobley is a perfect place to pause awhile on the Black & White Trail through Herefordshire, and the **Elizabethan Guest House** is ideal for that purpose. The friendly, caring owners are Janet and

Elizabethan Guest House, High Street, Weobley, Herefordshire HR4 8SL
Tel: 01544 318230

Eric Humphreys, and their guests include many professional people (lots of return visits) and tourists from home and abroad. The building - Grade ll* Listed - is 14th century, black and white of course, with an overhanging top storey, a tiled roof, and an oak front door. The three excellent letting bedrooms, all en suite, comprise a twin with bath and shower and two doubles with bath and shower attachment. The twin has two Victorian brass beds, one of the doubles is all pine and the other features a French rosewood bed with drapes, and period furniture. All have TVs and tea/coffee-makers. The whole place has been taste-fully refurbished, and beams add old-world appeal in the bedrooms and in the residents' lounge, where renovation work revealed an ancient stone fireplace hidden behind a 1950s front. The guest house is B&B only (a full English break-fast is served in the separate breakfast room) and is not licensed, but Weobley is not short of places for eating and drinking, including the Unicorn pub next door and the famous Ye Olde Salutation Inn.

ALMELEY   MAP 1 REF C10
5 miles W of Weobley Off the A480

A small village with many fine old timbered buildings, a handsome 15th-cen-tury manor house, a massive cruck-beamed barn (at Castle Froome Farm) and the 14th-century Church of St Mary with a sturdy tower and unusual painted roof. **Almeley Castle** was once the home of Sir John Oldcastle, a follower of Wycliffe and, it is thought, the model for Shakespeare's Falstaff.

KINNERSLEY   MAP 1 REF C10
5 miles SW of Weobley on the A4112

On the main road lie the village and **Kinnersley Castle**, which has the look of a fortified manor house. Famous occupants down the years include the Morgans (Sir Henry Morgan was one of them) and the Vaughans. Black Vaughan's huge dog is believed to have been the inspiration for Conan Doyle's *Hound of the Baskervilles*. The eight acres of grounds contain many fine specimen trees. Tel: 01544 327407.

EARDISLEY   MAP 1 REF C10
8 miles W of Weobley on the A4111

The greatest treasure of Eardisley's **Church of St Mary Magdalene** is its font, dating from the early 12th century. The figures depicted round the font repre-sent not only familiar religious themes but also two men in armed struggle. It is thought that these are a 12th-century lord of the manor, Ralph de Baskerville, and his father-in-law, whom he killed in a dispute over land. Outside the vil-lage, the most notable feature, standing majestically by an old chapel, is the **Great Oak**, which is probably 800 years old.

KINGTON

MAP 1 REF B9

12 miles W of Weobley on the A44

The road up to Kington passes many places of interest, and for two in particular a short pause will be well worth while. The National Trust's **Cwmmau Farmhouse**, which lies 4 miles south of Kington between the A4111 and A438 at **Brilley**, is an imposing timber-framed and stone-tiled farmhouse dating from the early 17th century. Viewing is by guided tour only. Tel: 01497 831251.

Half a mile off the A44 on the Welsh side of Kington are **Hergest Croft Gardens**, four distinct gardens that include rhododendrons up to 30' tall, spectacular azaleas, an old-fashioned kitched garden and a marvellous collection of trees and shrubs. Tel: 01544 230160

Nearby is the impressive **Hergest Ridge**, rising to around 1,400', and, on its southern edge, **Hergest Court**, once owned by the Vaughan family, whom we met at Kinnersley. Two members of the family who gained particular notoriety were Thomas 'Black' Vaughan and his wife, who was known as 'Gethen the Terrible'. She is said to have taken revenge on a man who killed her brother by taking part in an archery competition disguised as a man. When her turn came to compete, she shot him dead at point blank range and escaped in the ensuing melee. Thomas died at the Battle of Banbury in 1469, but, being a true Vaughan, that was not ther last of him. He is said to have haunted the church in the guise of a bull, and even managed to turn himself into a horsefly to annoy the local horses. He was back in taurine form when he was finally overcome by a band of clerics. One of the band managed to shrink him and cram him into a snuff box, which was quickly consigned to the waters of Hergest Pool. Later owners of the estate found and unwittingly opened the box, letting Black Vaughan loose once more. The next band of intrepid clerics confined the spirit under an oak tree, but he is currently at large again - though not sighted for many years. These feisty Vaughans are buried in the Vaughan Chapel in Kington parish church.

Kington itself lies on the England/Wales border and, like other towns in the area known as the Marches, had for many years to look closely to the west, whence the wild Welsh would attack. Kington's castle was destroyed many centuries ago, but outside the town, on **Wapley Hill**, are earthworks of an ancient hill fort which could be the site of King Caractacus' last stand.

Most notable by far of all the defences in the region is **Offa's Dyke**, the imposing ditch that extends for almost 180 miles along the border, from the Severn Estuary at Sedbury Cliffs near Chepstow, across the Black Mountain ridge, through the Wye Valley and north to Prestatyn on the North Wales coast. Offa was a Mercian king of great influence, with strong diplomatic links with the Popes and Charlemagne, who ruled the land south of the Humber from 757 to 796. Remnants of wooden stakes unearthed down the years suggest that the Dyke had a definite defensive role, rather than acting merely as a psychological barrier. It was a truly massive construction, in places almost 60' wide, and although nowadays it disappears in places, much of it can still be walked, particularly in the Wye Valley. A stretch north of Kington is especially well preserved and provides excellent, invigorating walking for the energetic. The walk crosses, at **Bradnor Hill**, the highest golf course, over 1200' above sea level. Other major traces of the Dyke remain, notably between Chepstow and Monmouth and by Oswestry, and at many points Offa's Dyke Path, opened by the Countryside Commission in 1971, diverts from the actual Dyke into magnificent scenery.

LYONSHALL
MAP 1 REF C10

15 miles W of Leominster on the A480

Church and castle remains are at some distance from the main body of the village, a fact which is often attributed to the plague causing older settlements to be abandoned. The Church of St Michael and All Angels dates mainly from the 13th century and was restored in 1870 when close to collapse. The ruins of the castle include some walls and part of the moat, making this the most 'complete' of all the castle ruins in the area. Among the fine old buildings in the village itself are the Royal George Inn, Ivy House, The Wharf and The Woodlands. There are two 12th-century watercorn mills in the parish, one of them, **Bullock's Mill**, being documented continuously from 1580 to 1928.

PEMBRIDGE
MAP 1 REF C9

10 miles W of Leominster on the A44

The influential Mortimer family were responsible for the medieval prosperity of

Pembridge Belfry

historic Pembridge, and many handsome buildings bear witness to their patronage and its legacy. The most famous building is the 14th-century church, a three-storey structure in stone and timber with a marvellous timber **belfry**. The bell and the clock mechanism can be viewed from inside the church. Two other buildings which the visitor should not miss are the delightful 16th-century **market hall** standing on its eight oak pillars and the **Old Chapel Gallery** in a converted Victorian chapel.

A little way south of Pembridge is **Dunkerton's Cider Mill**, where cider and perry are produced from organically grown local fruit. Tel: 01432 388653.

STAUNTON ON ARROW
10 miles W of Leominster on minor roads

MAP 1 REF C9

A mile north of Pembridge, across the River Arrow, Staunton is a most attractive village that enjoys particularly delightful views.

Tucked away in this most attractive village is a real gem - **Horseway Herbs**, run by Judy and Roger Davies. At Horseway Herbs, the ancient art of cultivating herbs is carried on in grounds absolutely full of herbs and flowers. You can buy all sorts of fresh-cut herbs, herb plants and herbal preparations while enjoying

**Horseway Herbs, Horseway Head Cottage, Staunton on Arrow,
Near Leominster, Herefordshire HR6 9HS Tel/Fax: 01544 388212**

the magical surroundings. You can also buy bedding plants and hanging baskets. There is a tea room housed in an old barn and we could not think of a more delightful way of spending some time than just relaxing and walking round the gardens enjoying the smells, with a cup of tea and a light snack before heading off again. A perfect spot, open 10-5 April-October daily except Wednesday. Admission free.

EARDISLAND

MAP 1 REF C9

8 miles W of Leominster on the B4529

"An uncommonly pretty village", said Pevsner of this renowned spot on the banks of the River Arrow. Certainly glorious Eardisland is one of the most beuatiful villages in the county (and the competition is very strong), and with its inns, bowling green, river and charming buildings spanning the centuries, this is essential England. Dominating the scene is the 12th-century **Church of St Mary**

Eardisland Bridge

the Virgin, where each year, from Easter until late autumn, an exhibition of village and parish life is staged. A mile outside the village is **Burton Court**, whose centrepiece is the sumptuous 14th-century Great Hall. Many additions have been made to the building down the years, and the present entrance, dating from 1912, is the work of Sir Clough Williams-Ellis of Portmeirion fame. Highlight of the various attractions is a collection of European and Oriental costumes, but of interest too are a model ship collection, a wide range of natural history specimens and a working model fairground. Also pick-your-own fruit. Tel: 01544 388231.

In the heart of one of the loveliest villages in the country, **The Manor House** is a beautiful 17th century house on the banks of the River Arrow. The gardens are an absolute picture, with a waterfall rolling in from the old mill race and an imposing Queen Anne dovecote recently restored to pristine splendour. A large sunny terrace is the perfect spot to unwind with a drink at the end of the day. In

The Manor House, Eardisland, Near Leominster, Herefordshire HR6 9BN
Tel: 01544 388138

this wonderful setting Carolin Lowry offers overnight accommodation in three beautifully furnished upstairs bedrooms, two en suite and the third with a very spacious private bathroom. Downstairs is a sitting room with a liberal supply of books, magazines amd games. Breakfast, either traditional English or Continental, is served in the dining room, where guests sit on Chippendale chairs among a profusion of antiques. Evening meals are not provided, but there are several excellent restaurants and pubs nearby. No smoking in the house. ETB 4 Diamond Rating.

3 South Worcestershire

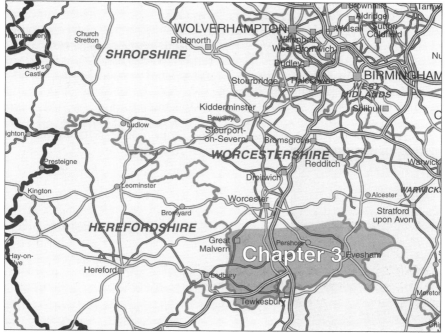

© MAPS IN MINUTES ™ (1998)

This chapter takes in the southern part of the county, starting with the spectacular ridge of the Malvern Hills in the west, with marvellous walking and breathtaking views. Moving eastwards, the route calls at Upton-upon-Severn, Pershore and Evesham, along with many charming villages and ancient sites. The Vale of Evesham, through which the Warwickshire countryside wanders, is one of the country's most important and prolific horticultural regions, and in springtime the Vale is alive with colour from the blossom of the fruit trees. High-quality fruit and vegetables are distributed from here throughout the land, and motorists will come across numerous roadside stalls selling a wonderful array of produce, At the eastern edge of this part of the county lies Broadway, a quintessential Cotswold village of outstanding beauty, beloved of tourists and not to be missed on any visit to this most delightful county.

GREAT MALVERN

Beneath the northeastern slopes of the **Malvern Hills**, Great Malvern is known for its porcelain, its annual music and drama festivals, Malvern water and Morgan cars. Though invaded by tourists for much of the year, Great Malvern has retained its dignity and elegance, with open spaces, leafy avenues and handsome houses. Close to the start of the Malvern walking trail, on a path leading up from the town, is a Regency cottage housing one source of the water – **St Anne's Well** – where one can sample the water and drink in the views. Great Malvern was for many centuries a quiet, little-known place with a priory at its heart, and even when the curative properties of its spring waters were discovered, it took a long time for it to become a fashionable spa resort. Hotels, baths and a pump room were built in the early 19th century, and the arrival of the railway provided easy access from the middle of the century. The station is one of many charming Victorian buildings, and with its cast-iron pillars, stone ornaments and beautifully painted floral designs, is a tourist attraction in its own right.

On the platform of Great Malvern railway station, **Lady Foley's Tea Room** is not only a haven for train passengers but also a great favourite with the residents of Malvern. Elegantly restored in Victorian style, Margaret Baddeley's tea room provides excellent hot and cold snacks and a variety of teas, coffees, hot chocolate and cold drinks. Sandwiches and rolls, scones, salad platters, quiche

Lady Foley's Tea Room, Great Malvern Station, Imperial Road, Malvern, Worcestershire WR14 3AT Tel: 01684 893033

and baked potatoes are supplemented by daily specials. Adjoining the tea room is a craft shop selling quality gifts made by local crafts people. The station itself is well worth a look: it has been restored to its Victorian splendour, but no longer boasts the furnished room which Lady Foley, a local landowner who was largely responsible for the planning of Malvern, would use while waiting for her train to London. The pillars supporting the platform roof are of particular interest, their tops depicting various local flora.

Oswald and Karen Dockery took over the ownership of the **Malvern Hills Hotel** at the end of 1997, having spent six years running a very successful hotel in Gloucestershire. Their current enterprise is a 19th century building in the heart of the Malverns, 800 feet above sea level and a great base for walkers or centre for touring. Overnight accommodation comprises 15 well-equipped bedrooms, all en suite, and most enjoying views over either the tranquil Herefordshire countryside or British Camp, one of the best preserved Iron Age

**The Malvern Hills Hotel, Wynds Point, Malvern,
Worcestershire WR13 6DW Tel: 01684 540690**

hill forts in the land. The hotel has two bars, one oak-panelled and named after Jenny Lind, whose house is next door, the other in contemporary style. Nightingales Restaurant is an elegant dining room where chef Paul Haywood offers his own rustic English style of cooking, with influences from around the world: pea and ham soup with truffle oil; braised lamb shank with glazed button onions and pickled beetroot; crisp-fried fillet of Cornish cod on a tomato, aubergine and potato salad; pear tarte tatin with caramel sauce and vanilla ice cream; warm chocolate tart with lemon mascarpone. Garden with tables and chairs; large car park. Children and pets welcome.

The Priory **Church of St Mary and St Michael** is a dominant feature in the centre of the town. Its windows, the west a gift from Richard lll, the east from Henry Vll, contain a wonderful collection of 15th-century stained glass, and another unique feature is a collection of more than 1,200 wall tiles on the chancel screens. These also date from the 15th century. Among many interesting graves in the cemetery is that of Jenny Lind, 'The Swedish Nightingale', who was born in Stockholm in 1820 and died at Wynd's Point, Malvern which she used as a summer retreat, in 1887. In the churchyard at West Malvern Peter Mark Roget (the Thesaurus man) is buried (interred, entombed, coffined, laid to rest, consigned to earth). The 14th-century **Abbey Gateway**, whose huge wooden gateposts can be seen in the archway, houses the **Malvern Museum** (Tel: 01684 567811). Open Easter

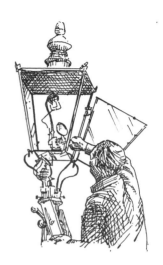

Malvern Gas Lamps

to October, it displays include the geology of the Malvern Hills, the history of Malvern spring water and the development of Morgan cars. In Tanhouse Lane stands the factory of Boehm of Malvern, where the remarkable American Edward Marshall Boehm (call it 'Beam') founded the centre which has become known worldwide for the quality of its porcelain. Great Malvern has a distinguished tradition of arts and culture, much of it the legacy of Sir Edward Elgar and George Bernard Shaw, and the **Victorian Winter Gardens** are an exciting setting for performances of music and drama. Malvern is the home of the excellent English Symphony Orchestra, formed in 1980 by William Boughton.

Great Malvern is the largest of six settlements that make up the Malverns: to the south are Malvern Wells and Little Malvern, to the north North Malvern and to the northeast Malvern Link. A

English Symphony Orchestra, Malvern

permanent site on low ground below Great Malvern is the venue for the **Three Counties Show**, one of England's premier agricultural shows.

The Three Horseshoes stands on Poolbrook Common only half a mile from the Three Counties Showground, where one of the country's leading agricultural events is held each June. Originally two Victorian cottages, it has been a pub since the turn of the century, and its prime position makes it very popular with both locals and visitors. Graham and Jill Smith run it with their daughter, and it's very much the centre of community life, with teams for dominoes, crib and quizzes, and occasional live music. Outside are hanging baskets and a col-

The Three Horseshoes, 105 Poolbrook Road, Poolbrook, Near Malvern, Worcestershire WR14 3JW Tel: 01684 573983

ourful garden; inside, plenty of space and comfort, an open fire and a large collection of jugs. Quality cask ales take care of dry throats, while for hungry visitors Jill and her chef prepare a good range of food, from sandwiches and snacks to home-made paté, lasagne, gammon, baltis and a variety of other dishes. In the evening the choice extends to savoury pies, mixed grills, steaks, fish and vegetarian meals.

A cheerful black and white facade welcomes visitors to **The Green Dragon**, a popular place to pause on the B4211 Malvern-Upton road. Mark and Sue Jones have been here for 12 years, so they certainly know their regulars, who include two football teams, an arts club and a group of teachers. There's also a steady stream of tourists, who, like the locals, appreciate the peaceful, relaxed atmos-

**The Green Dragon, 126 Guarlford Road, Malvern,
Worcestershire WR14 3QT Tel: 01684 572350**

phere, the freshly prepared home-cooked food (Mark is the chef) and the home-brewed beers called Downfall and Revenge. Coffee and tea are also available. Inside the pub, pictures of yesteryear adorn the panelled walls, while at the back is a well-laid flower garden, along with a beer garden and children's play area. The pub has a large car park.

Set in 17 acres of spectacular countryside two miles from Malvern on the western edge of the Malvern Hills, **Runnings Park** is a leading centre for health, healing and self-development. Peace and tranquillity are guaranteed, and the views are truly inspiring, stretching over 30 miles down the valley to the Black Mountains. Individuals and groups come from the UK and all over the world to recharge their batteries and enjoy the centre's harmonious blend of inspiration and balance. At the Health and Relaxation Centre they specialise in treatments for the whole person, mind and body, with the programme tailored to fit individual needs. The treatments include massage, aromatherapy, reflexology, floatation, counselling, hypnotherapy, nutritional therapy and healing. Guests can take plenty of time to unwind and relax, and apart from the treatments the centre has a sauna and a swimming pool. Accommodation comprises 26 simple, cosy bedrooms, most of them en suite, with TV, telephone and tea/coffee-mak-

Runnings Park, Croft Bank, West Malvern, Worcestershire WR14 4DU
Tel: 01684 573868 Fax: 01684 892047

ing facilities. The inner man is not forgotten, and in the stylish Sanctuary Restaurant an award-winning chef caters for all tastes and most dietary requirements, using as much organic produce as possible in his dishes. Typical choices on his innovative, well-balanced, three-course dinner menu are mangetout and lemon soup; steamed supreme of Scottish salmon with a dressing of olives, sun-dried tomatoes and coriander; noisettes of English lamb napped with a port and red-currant sauce; and mushroom and celery charlotte with a stir-fry of peppers. To finish, perhaps a sweet omelette with mixed berries served on a fruit purée, or a selection of English cheeses. Lunch is a lighter, two-course buffet.

Runnings Park caters well for individuals but is also a highly successful training and conference centre with a unique range of training courses focused on the health, well-being and development of individuals and the business teams they work in. The Park was built at the end of the 19th century by Lady Howard de Walden as a model dairy farm and was converted to its present use in 1981. Directors David Balen and Tony Neate are in charge of a team whose expertise, friendliness and desire to help makes Runnings Park such a special place.

LITTLE MALVERN
MAP 4 REF G11
4 miles S of Great Malvern on the A449

At Little Malvern stands the **Church of St Wulstan**, where a simple headstone marks the grave of Sir Edward Elgar and his wife Caroline. Their daughter is buried next to them.

Little Malvern Court, off the A4104, enjoys a glorious setting on the lower slopes of the Malvern Hills. It stands next to **Little Malvern Priory**, whose hall, the only part that survived the Dissolution, is now incorporated into the Court. Of the priory church, only the chancel tower and south transept remain. The Court was once a Catholic safe house, with a chapel reached by a secret staircase. The Court and gardens are open Wednesday and Thursday afternoons from mid-April to mid-July.

Just to the north at **Malvern Wells**, where the first medicinal wells were discovered, stands St Peter's Church, dating from 1836 and notable for some original stained glass and a William Morris window of 1885.

MALVERN LINK
Map 4 ref G10
1 mile NW of Great Malvern on the A449

Rosita's Thai Restaurant is a single-storey brick-and-glass building adorned with a variety of plants, set in a quiet courtyard just off the main Malvern-Worcester road and very near the Morgan car factory. It started life three years ago as a coffee shop with theme nights, and since the Thai nights were the most popular, Rosita Bowcutt decided to turn it into a full-time Thai restaurant. In bright, relaxed surroundings, her Thai chef produces a menu that includes the classics that have become so popular with the British dining public: tod mun pla (fish cakes), satay, tom yum soup, roast duck, stir-fries and curries whose colour indi-

**Rosita's Thai Restaurant, 8 Fir Tree Walk, 134 Worcester Road,
Malvern Link, Worcestershire WR14 1SS Tel: 01684 891217**

cates the heat level - yellow, red or green. There are plenty of vegetarian choices, among them noodle dishes and 'Rosita's Favourite', which is grilled aubergine slices dipped in a spicy, herby egg mixture and shallow-fried in sesame oil. Opening times are 12-2 Tuesday-Friday & 6.30-10.30 Tuesday-Saturday.

AROUND THE MALVERNS

The whole area is glorious walking country, with endless places to discover and explore. **British Camp**, on Herefordshire Beacon 2 miles west of Little Malvern, is one of the most important Roman settlements in Britain, and a little way south is **Midsummer Hill**, site of another ancient settlement. Six miles south of Great Malvern on the B4208 is the **Malvern Hills Animal and Bird Garden**, whose collection of animals includes snakes, monkeys and wallabies (Tel: 01684 310016).

COLWALL

MAP 4 REF G11

2 miles SW of Great Malvern off the B4218

On the west side of the Malverns, Colwall lies just across the border in Herefordshire. Its chief claim to fame is the enormous lump of limestone which stands at its centre. How it got there no one knows, but the Devil and a local giant are among the suspects. Less mysterious are the attractions of the **Picton Garden**, which contains a National Collection of Michaelmas daisies, which flower in September/October (Tel: 01684 540416). William Langland, author of *Piers Plowman*, lived at Colwall.

BIRTSMORTON

MAP 4 REF G11

7 miles S of Great Malvern off the B4208

In the Church of St Peter and St Paul are monuments to the Nanfan family, owners of the nearby **Birtsmorton Court**. Other notable residents of this magnificent building (not open to the public) include William Huskisson, who in 1830 became the first person to be killed in a railway accident.

HANLEY CASTLE

MAP 4 REF G11

6 miles SE of Great Malvern on the B4209

The village takes its name from the castle, which was originally a hunting lodge for King John, and which disappeared , except for its moat, many centuries ago. There's still plenty to see in this attractive little spot, including picturesque cottages, a 16th-century grammar school and the Church of St Mary in stone and brick.

The castle has long since gone, but the village remains, and among its many attractive buildings one of the most appealing is the **Three Kings Inn** with its sign of the Three Wise Men. This is an unspoilt 15th century inn, a total delight

Three Kings Inn, Hanley Castle, Worcestershire, WR8 0BL
Tel: 01684 592686

both inside and out. Behind the facade, part brick, part timbered, the bars are perhaps the most atmospheric you will ever encounter, with beams, brasses and inglenook fireplaces adorned with an array of old ornaments and fires blazing under copper hoods. The pub is a mecca for real ale fans and has regularly featured in the lists of CAMRA prizewinners, including National Pub of the Year in 1993 and runner-up in 1998. The regular Butcombe and Thwaites ales are joined by three others from small independent breweries, including perhaps Thirsty Willie's Bitter and Malvern Hills Black Pear. The hungry are also well catered for, with anything from a light snack to grills, chicken Kiev, salmon en croute and three Wellingtons: classic beef, salmon & halibut, and Provençal nut. Live music Sunday evenings, sing-alongs alternate Saturday evenings. Sheila Roberts, here since the early 1960s, runs this wonderful place with her daughter Sue, and the family have been here since 1911.

UPTON-ON-SEVERN   Map 4 ref G11
7 miles SE of Great Malvern on the A4104

An unspoilt town which gained prominence as one of the few bridging points on the Severn. The first records indicate that it was a Roman station, and it is mentioned in the Domesday Book. It became an important medieval port, and its strategic position led to its playing a role in the Civil War. In 1651, Charles sent a force to Upton to destroy the bridge, but after a long and bloody struggle the King's troops were routed and Cromwell regained the town. A Dutch gabled building used for stabling during the War still stands. The medieval church, one of the most distinctive buildings in the whole county, is affectionately known as **'the Pepperpot'**, because of its handsome tower with its copper-covered cupola, the work the 18th-century architect Keek. This former place of worship is now a heritage centre, telling of the Civil War battles and the town's history. The Church of St Peter and St Paul, built in 1879, has an interesting talking point in a large metal abstract hanging above the altar. **The Tudor House**, which contains a museum of Upton past and present, is open daily on summer after-noons. The **White Lion Hotel**, in the High Street, has a history going back to 1510 and was the setting for some scenes in Henry Fielding's *Tom Jones*. The commecial trade has largely left the Severn, replaced by a steadt stream of sum-mertime pleasure craft.

Owner Jane Holder's hobby is cooking, so visitors to **Katie's Coffee Shop** can look forward to a real treat when they drop in for a snack. Cosy and charm-ingly furnished, with beams and a Welsh dresser, it was built in the 16th century as a workhouse, and now forms part of a row of retail outlets in a narrow street

Katie's Coffee Shop, 11 Court Street, Upton-on-Severn,
Worcestershire WR8 0JS Tel: 01684 592097

near the centre of this pretty riverside town. The Big Breakfast provides excellent fuel for walkers and cyclists discovering a lovely part of the world, and throughout the day sandwiches plain or toasted, salads, filled jacket potatoes and omelettes fit the bill in fine style. Bread pudding, teacakes, apple pie and home-made cakes cater admirably for the sweeter tooth.

AROUND UPTON-ON-SEVERN

RIPPLE   Map 4 ref G11
4 miles S of Upton off the A38

The village square is tiny, making the Church of St Mary seem even larger than it is. Note the misericords showing the Labours of the Seasons.

EARLS CROOME   Map 4 ref H11
2 miles E of Upton on the A4104

There are several attractions in the area of Earls Croome. **Croome Landscape Park**, under the care of the National Trust, was Capability Brown's first complete landscape, which made his reputation and set a pattern for parkland design that lasted half a century. The buildings have equally distinguished pedigrees, with Robert Adam and James Wyatt as architects. Tel: 01905 371006

Dunstall Castle Folly

The **Hill Croome Dovecote** is a very rare square building next to the church in Hill Croome. **Dunstall Castle** folly at **Dunstall Common** is a folly in the style of a Norman castle, put up in the 18th century and comprising two round towers and one square, connected by arches.

Originally tied cottages on the Earl's Croome estate, **The Jockey Inn** is a neat, whitewashed building on the A4104 a mile and a half out of Upton. Self-catering accommodation for up to four guests is available, but this is first and foremost an eating pub, and landlord Peter Lee is a trained chef. The setting is

The Jockey Inn, Baughton, Earl's Croome, Near Upton-upon-Severn, Worcestershire WR8 9DQ Tel: 01684 592153

civilised and comfortable - original beams, subdued lighting, pictures, brass ornaments - and very appropriate for the high-quality cuisine on offer. The menu takes its inspiration from near and far, with such dishes as deep-fried brie with Cumberland sauce, chicken satay and filo-wrapped prawns among the starters. Typical main dishes might include duck breast in a Pimm's and redcurrant glaze, salmon fillet in lemon and herb butter, and a speciality dish of pan-fried beef fillets served in large field mushrooms and covered with a sauce of bourbon, cracked peppercorns and cream. The accompanying selection of fresh vegetables changes daily - another example of how seriously food is taken at this excellent place. To round things off in style are some fairly wicked puddings such as treacle and orange tart drizzled with Cointreau.

At **Croome d'Abitot**, a little way north of Earls Croome, the 18th-century Church of St Mary Magdalene is filled with memorials to the Coventry family – it stood on their estate.

PERSHORE
MAP 4 REF H10
6 miles NE of Upton on the A4104

A gem of a market town, with fine Georgian architecture and an attractive setting on the banks of the Avon. Its crowning glory is the **Abbey**, combining outstanding examples of Norman and Early English architecture. The Abbey was founded by King Oswald in 689, and in 972 King Edgar granted a charter to the Benedictine monks. Only the choir remains of the original church, but it is still a considerable architectural treasure. The south transept is the oldest part, while among the most impressive features is some superb vaulting in the chancel roof.

Pershore Bridge, a favourite picnic spot, still bears the marks of damage done during the Civil War. A mile east of town on the A44 is Pershore College of Architecture. Originally part of the Wyke Estate, the college has been developed round an early 19ᵗʰ-century mansion and is the Royal Horticultural Society's Centre for the West Midlands. The ground contains many unusual trees and shrubs, and in the glasshouses are tropical, temperate and cool decorative plants.

Pershore Abbey

AROUND PERSHORE

ECKINGTON
Map 4 ref H11

4 miles SW of Pershore on the B4080

The small village of Eckington can be traced back to 172AD; it was originally a Roman settlement on land belonging to the British tribe of Dobuni. The bridge over the Avon, which dates from the 15ᵗʰ century, has an adjacent car park which is a popular picnic site.

Beacon's Nurseries have built up a reputation for quality, reliability and value for money over the past 35 years. The range of plants for sale is enormous, with well over 1,000 varieties available at any one time, almost all grown by the Beacons (John, Jonathan and Linda) on 13 acres of land. Shrubs, climbing plants, conifers, roses and camellias fill a substantial catalogue, with a wide range of perennials and water plants available in addition. Each plant sold is labelled

with a description and indication of any special requirements. Additional advice is given willingly. The owners are continually assessing plants and looking for new and improved varieties. They have recently introduced *"Ceanothus thyrsiflorus"* Borne Again, with pale blue flowers in spring and autumn and a broad golden leaf margin. Display gardens are being developed. An attraction for younger visitors is a miniature railway that runs on Saturday afternoons. Open 9-1 & 2-5 Monday-Saturday, 2-5 Sunday.

Beacon's Nurseries, Tewkesbury Road, Eckington, Near Pershore, Worcestershire, WR10 3DE Tel: 01386 750359

The area south of Pershore towards the boundary with Gloucestershire is dominated by **Bredon Hill**, which is surrounded by charming villages such as Great and Little Comberton and Elmley Castle on the north side, and Bredon, Overbury and Kennerton to the south. Bredon Hill is almost circular, a limestone outcrop of the Cotswolds covering 12 square miles, accessible from many of the villages that ring it, and rising to over 900'. On the crest of its northern slope, best accessed from Great Comberton, are the remains – part of the earthworks – of the pre-Roman settlement known as Kennerton Camp. Much more visible on the top is a curious brick tower called Parsons Folly, built by a Mr Parsons in the 18th century.

ELMLEY CASTLE
MAP 4 REF H11
5 miles SE of Pershore on a minor road

Just one of the many enchanting villages around Bredon Hill, no longer boasting a castle but with this memorandum of 1540: *"The late Castle of Elmley standing on high and adjoining the Park, compassed in with wall and ditch is uncovered and in decay."*

The village's main street is very wide and lined with trees, with a little brook flowing to one side. Picturesque cottages with thatched roofs lead up to a well-preserved 15th-century cross, then to St Mary's Church with its handsome tower and battlements. Inside are some of the finest monuments to be found anywhere in England, most notably the 17th-century alabaster tomb of William Savage, his son Giles and Giles's wife and children.

BREDON
MAP 4 REF H11
6 miles S of Pershore off the B4080

Plenty to see in this sizeable village, notably the Church of St Giles with its 14th-century stained glass and some very elaborate stone monuments; an Elizabethan rectory with stone figures on horseback on the roof; and some fine 18th-century stables. **Bredon Barn**, owned by the National Trust, is a huge 14th-century barn built of local Cotswold stone. 132' in length, it has a dramatic aisled interior, marvellous beams and two porches at the wagon entrances. Open April-November. Tel: 01684 850051.

WYRE PIDDLE
MAP 4 REF H10
2 miles NE of Pershore on the A4538

Rest, comfort and tranquillity are guaranteed to guests at **Arbour House**, a fine Grade ll Listed house with flagstone floors, oak beams and real fires. Originally built as labourers' cottages in the 1550s, it became the prosperous George Inn serving the boat hauliers on the banks of the Avon. By 1890 it had again become a private residence, and Pat and Phil Jennings have been offering bed & breakfast accommodation since 1996. The three comfortable rooms - a double and two twins - have en suite bath or shower, central heating, TVs, tea-makers,

**Arbour House Bed & Breakfast, Main Road, Wyre Piddle,
Worcestershire WR10 2HU Tel: 01386 555833**

radio-alarms, hairdryers and shoe-cleaning kits. The dining room, which is heated by a wood-burning stove in an inglenook fireplace, is adorned with a collection of plates, pictures and curios. Guests can relax in the lounge with a good selection of books and games. A full English breakfast uses the very best of local produce, and packed lunches and evening meals can be provided with advance notice. The house has a small garden and overlooks open meadows, with fine views towards Bredon Hill. No children under 10 except babes in arms. No pets. No smoking.

PEOPLETON
Map 4 ref H10

5 miles N of Pershore off the A4538

Highlight of the year in this village is the Gymkhana, Dog Show and Clay-Pigeon Shoot, which takes place towards the end of May at Lower Norchard Farm.

Andy and Pauline Taynton provide a friendly greeting for regulars and first-timers at the delightful old **Crown Inn**. Children and dogs are included in the welcome, and the pub is a meeting place for cricket and football teams as well as the scene of some stirring games of cards, darts and dominoes. Clay-pigeon shooting can be arranged nearby. Real ales accompany a good choice of eating, from a light lunch menu of sandwiches, ploughman's platters and jacket pota-

The Crown Inn, Peopleton, Near Pershore, Worcestershire WR10 2EE
Tel: 01905 840222

toes to full meals. The scene inside is pleasingly traditional, with brasses, an old gun over the inglenook fireplace and pictures of days of yore in the neighbourhood. A jukebox-free zone, but the pub holds occasional live music evenings.

WICK
MAP 4 REF H11

1 mile E of Pershore on the A44

Just beyond the College of Horticulture on the road to Evesham, Wick has a fine little church of Norman origin, and a handsome manor house in Jacobean style but dating only from the 1920s.

FLADBURY
MAP 4 REF I10

4 miles E of Pershore off the A4538/A44

On the banks of the Avon, whose waters powered the old mill for many centuries. Exceptional pieces in the Church of St John the Baptist include memorial brasses to the Throckmorton family, shields of Henry lll and Simon de Montfort and some fine stained glass.

EVESHAM
MAP 4 REF I11

7 miles SE of Pershire on the A44

A bustling market town at the centre of the Vale of Evesham, an area long known as the Garden of England, with a prolific harvest of soft fruits, apples, plums and salad vegetables. The **Blossom Trail**, which starts in the town, is a popular outing when the fruit trees burst into blossom. The Trail follows a signposted route from the High Street to Greenhill, where the Battle of Evesham took place. The River Avon performs a loop round the town, and the Abbey park is a good place for a riverside stroll; it is also the start point for boat trips. The magnificent bell tower (110') is the only major building remaining of the **Abbey**, which was built around 700 by Egwin, Bishop of Worcester, and was one of the largest and grandest in the whole country. It was knocked down by Henry Vlll's men at the time of the Dissolution of the Monasteries. The story of the town is told in vivid detail at the **Almonry Heritage Centre**, which was formerly the home of the Abbey Almoner and was built around 1400. It now houses a unique collection of artifacts as well as exhibitions showing the history of the Abbey, and the defeat of Simon de Montfort at the Battle of Evesham in 1265 (the Leicester Tower stands on the site of the Battle). The Almonry also houses Evesham's Tourist Information Centre.

There are many other interesting buildings in Evesham, including the neighbouring churches of All Saints and St Lawrence. The former is entered through a porch built by Abbot Lichfield in the 16th century, and the Lichfield Chapel, with a lovely fan-vaulted ceiling, contains his tomb. Much of the building, as well as the stone pulpit, dates from Victorian times, when major restoration work was carried out. The latter, declared redundant in 1978, was also the subject of extensive restoration, in the 1830s and again in the 1990s. In the market place is a grand old timbered building called the **Round House** – a curious name, because it is actually square.

AROUND EVESHAM

A little way north of Evesham is Twyford Country Centre, where all kinds of plants and garden equipment can be bought, along with craftwork and antiques. There's a farm shop and café on the site, along with a picnic area leading to footpaths by the river.

BADSEY   MAP 4 REF I11
2 miles E of Evesham off the B4035

The Church of St James is the spiritual centre of this village, where Roman coins and pottery have been unearthed. Badsey is in the heart of asparagus country.

Ken and Heather Woods took over the reins at **The Wheatsheaf Inn** at the beginning of 1999 on their return from South Africa, where they had spent 16 years. The Wheatsheaf is a handsome row of linked 17th century stone buildings, whitewashed and under slate roofs. It stands in a quiet village on the

**The Wheatsheaf Inn, 29 High Street, Badsey, Near Evesham,
Worcestershire WR11 5EW Tel: 01386 830380**

Broadway side of Evesham in an area renowned for its asparagus. Locals share the lively, relaxed atmosphere with walkers and tourists, and the pub also attracts nearby companies and the Round Table (a 50-seat function room is available for private meetings or parties). The bar is traditional in its appeal, with beams, flagstone floor and exposed stone walls hung with pictures. In the 40-cover dining room, freshly prepared food is served (the choice is marked up on a blackboard), accompanied by well-kept real ales. When the weather is kind, the picnic-style benches set out at the front and the courtyard at the rear come into their own. This sociable pub fields two darts teams, a crib team and a quiz team.

BRETFORTON
MAP 4 REF J11

4 miles E of Evesham on the B4035

A pub in the care of the National Trust is a rarity indeed, and it's well worth a trip to Bretforton to visit the **The Fleece Inn**, a medieval half-timbered that was originally a farmhouse. It has changed very little since being first licensed in 1848, and an interesting feature is the Witches' Marks carved in the hearth to prevent witches coming down the chimney. The Church of St Leonard boasts a number of interesting and intricate carvings, notably a scene depicting St Margaret emerging (through a hole she made with her cross) from the side of the dragon who has just swallowed her.

HONEYBOURNE
MAP 4 REF J11

5 miles E of Evesham on minor roads off the B4035

The Domestic Fowl Trust and Honeybourne Rare Breeds is a conservation centre for pure breeds of poultry and rare breeds of farm animals. All are in labeled breeding paddocks, and visitors are welcome to "stroke the sheep and say hello to the cows". Books, gifts and animal equipment and feedstuffs are available from the shop, and the centre also has a tea room.

MIDDLE LITTLETON
MAP 4 REF I10

3 miles NE of Evesham off the B4085

The Littletons – North, Middle and South – lie close to each other and close to the River Avon. In Middle Littleton is a huge and wonderful **tithe barn**, built in the 13th century and once the property of the Abbots of Evesham. Now owned by the National Trust, it is still in use as a farm building, but can be visited (Tel: 01684 850051).

Nearby, a bridleway leads off the B4510 to **Windmill Hill Nature Reserve**, an area of fertile limestone which continues up to Cleeve Prior, where the Church of St Andrew is well worth a visit.

HARVINGTON
Map 4 ref I10
3 miles N of Evesham on the B4088

A sizeable village with some attractive old cottages surrounding the Church of St James, in whose nave is a roll of honour with photographs of all the fighting men.

CHILDSWICKHAM
Map 4 ref I11
4 miles SE of Evesham off the A44

The **Church of St Mary the Virgin**, its tall, slender spire a prominent landmark, is a good place to start a walk round the old part of the village. Close by, on the Broadway roda, is the **Barnfield Cider Mill Museum**, where visitors can see a display of cider-making down the years before sampling cider, perry or one of the wines produced from local plums and berries. Tel: 01386 853145.

BROADWAY
Map 4 ref I11
6 miles S of Evesham on the A44

One of the most beautiful villages in England, and a magnet for tourists throughout the year. The quintessential Cotswold village, its eponymous broad main street is lined with houses and cottages built of golden Cotswold stone. Broadway was settled as far back as 1900BC, and later the Romans came and occupied the hill above the village. Broadway was probably re-established after the Battle of Dyrham in 557AD by conquering Saxons advancing towards Worcester. The parish records tell of hospitality being offered at a Broadway hostelry as early as 1532. This the time of the advent of the horse-drawn carriage, when Broadway became an important staging post. A journey from London to Worcester took about 17 hours including stops and a change of horse, and at one time Broadway boasted an incredible 33 public houses.

One of the must-sees on any trip to Broadway is the enchanting **Teddy Bear Museum**, housed in a picturesque 18th-century shop in the High Street. The atmosphere within is of an Edwardian carnival, with music playing, rides revolving and many other surprises. The hall of fame tells of celebrity bears, including Paddington, Pooh and the three who came upon Goldilocks. Bears of all ages and sizes are kept in stock, and some bears and dolls are made on the premises. Old bears and dolls are lovingly restored at – wait for it – St Beartholomew's Hospital. Tel: 01386 858323.

In the centre of Broadway is a wide village green from where the main street continues gently upwards for nearly a mile, with the surrounding hills always in view. The gradient increases at Fish Hill then rises to more than 1,000 feet above sea level at **Broadway Beacon**. At the top of the Beacon is **Broadway Tower**, standing in a delightful country park with something to interest all

Broadway Tower

ages, from animal enclosures and adventure playground to nature walks and barbecue sites. The tower was built as a folly by the 6th Earl of Coventry at the end of the 18th century as part of the great movement of the time towards picturesque and romantic landscapes. James Wyatt designed the tower, which now contains various displays and exhibitions.

Broadway's St Michael's Church (1839) boasts an intricate Elizabethan pulpit which came from the nearby St Eadburga's Church and was installed in a thanksgiving service marking the end of World War 1.

Dormy House Hotel can be found adjacent to Broadway Golf Club. For the uninitiated, 'dormy' in golfing terms means 'unbeatable', and that is a very fair description of this fine hotel, which offers visitors the opportunity to relax in superb surroundings. Everything about Dormy House is tasteful. The bedrooms are all en suite and attractively furnished with a mixture of antique and traditional pieces that lend charm to the rooms. Each bedroom has tea and coffee-making facilities, colour TV with teletext, radio-alarm, trouser press, hairdryer and direct-dial telephone; there is also a baby-listening service, which is always a boon to parents.

You can dine by candlelight in one of the prettiest restaurants we have ever seen, which is broken up into a series of small, intimate areas. The linen is in lovely pastel shades of beige and cream, and every table has fresh flowers. In such a relaxing atmosphere you feel absolutely right to enjoy the very best of English and French cuisine. You could perhaps start your meal with quenelles of Cornish turbot and Scottish salmon with a shellfish risotto and a chervil butter sauce and follow it with roast supreme of Barbary duckling with a duck confit potato cake on a red wine and star anise sauce. These are just two from a range of six starters and six main courses on the à la carte menu. There is also a table

Dormy House Hotel, Willersley Hill, Broadway, Worcestershire WR12 7LF
Tel: 01386 852711 Fax: 01386 858636

d'hote menu which changes daily. The choice is hard to make, and care is taken to ensure that you can have, for example, simply grilled or steamed fish if your diet demands it. With every main course comes a selection of fresh seasonal vegetables, which arrive at the table cooked to perfection. Follow this with one of the delectable sweets, or cheese from the English cheeseboard, and you will leave the table replete and happy. The fine wine list reflects the quality of the food and includes some superb vintages.

Dormy House is perfectly situated for anyone wanting to tour the Cotswolds, or the Herefordshire and Worcestershire areas. We think it is an excellent choice for visitors from overseas, because it is a hotel that upholds all that is best about English hospitality.

4 Central Worcestershire & Worcester

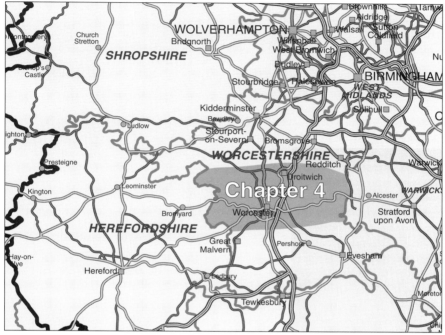

© MAPS IN MINUTES ™ (1998)

WORCESTER

This chapter takes Worcester as its base. Set on either side of the curving River Severn, Worcester is a bustling county capital and cathedral city. Its architecture spans many centuries and there are some marvellous examples from all of them. In the heart of England, this is an area characterised by red earth, apple orchards, hopyards, quiet inns, stone farmhouses and black-and-white timbered dwellings. As a visible legacy of the ancient forest that once surrounded Worcester, the half-timbered buildings lend colour and variety to the villages around this historic city.

The Cathedral, with its 200' tower, stands majestically beside the Severn. The 11th-century crypt is a classic example of Norman architecture and was built by St Wulstan, who is remembered in a stone carving. He was the only

English bishop not to be replaced by a Norman after the Conquest. To many of the local people the task of building the Cathedral must have seemed endless; the central tower collapsed in 1175 and a fire destroyed much of the building in 1203. The Cathedral had only just been re-dedicated after these disasters when Bishop Blois began pulling it down again, only to rebuild it in the fashionable Gothic style. The nave was rebuilt in the 14th century under the auspices of Bishop Cobham, but the south side was not completed until much later, and in a far less elaborate style. King John requested that he be buried in the choir, and his tomb stands near the high altar. It is a masterpiece of medieval sculpture, showing the King flanked by the Bishops Oswald and Wulstan. Prince Arthur, elder brother of Henry Vlll, is also entombed near the high altar.

River Severn at Worcester

There's a great deal more to see than the Cathedral, of course, and in the **City Museum and Art Gallery** (Tel 01905 25371) are contemporary art and archaeological displays, a 19th-century chemist's shop and the military collections of the Worcestershire Regiment and the Worcestershire Yeomanry Cavalry. Friar Street has many lovely old timber houses. **Greyfriars**, in the care of the National Trust, is a medieval house that has managed to survive right in the heart of the city, and passing through its archway visitors will come across a pretty walled garden. The imposing Guildhall in the High Street is a marvelous example of Queen Anne architecture, designed by a local man, Thomas White. **The Commandery Civil War Centre** (Tel 01905 355071) is a stunning complex of buildings behind a small timber-framed entrance. At the Battle of Worcester in 1651 the Commandery was used as the Royalist headquarters, and today period rooms offer a fascinating glimpse of the architecture and style of Tudor and Stuart times while acting as the country's only museum devoted to the story of the Civil War. The story takes in the trial of Charles l, visits a Royalist encampment on the eve of the battle and enacts the last battle of the war narrated by Charles ll and Oliver Cromwell.

The Commandery Civil War Centre, Worcester

The **Royal Worcester Porcelain** Visitor Centre (Tel 01905 23221) is an absolute must on any sightseer's list. Royal Worcester is Britain's oldest continuous producer of porcelain and is world famous for its exquisite bone china. The factory was founded in 1751 by Dr John Wall with the intention of creating *" a ware of a form so precise as to be easily distinguished from other English porcelain"*. The collection in the Museum contains some of the finest treasures of the factory, and visitors can take a guided tour of the factory to observe the many stages of production and the premises include a shop and a restaurant, where the food is naturally served on Royal Worcester china. In the 1930s the company was acquired by (Charles William) Dyson Perrins, the grandson of William Perrins, founder of the Worcester Sauce company.

The Lansdowne Inn is a new venture for experienced Debbie and John Curtis, who carried out major redecoration when they arrived in 1998. The building is late Victorian, with an old-world facade and a patio at the back with slides for children. Inside, the scene is set by beams and ornamental brasses, and there's an interesting collection of old programmes and other memorabilia associated with rugby union. Bar food, all freshly prepared, comprises snacks at lunchtime and early-evening suppers. Sunday lunch is very popular, and all

The Lansdowne Inn, Lansdowne Street, Worcester,
Worcestershire WR1 1QD Tel: 01905 28615

meals should end with the scrumptious apple pie and custard. The pub stands
behind the Royal Grammar School half a mile from the centre in the Lansdowne
district. The Worcester-Birmingham Canal is close by, and water-borne tourists
join the locals in spring and summer. Music nights once a month.

The **Museum of Local Life** (Tel 01905 722349) reflects the history of Worcester and its people, with displays covering the past 700 years. There's a Victorian
kitchen scene, a turn-of-the-century schoolroom and a variety of changing exhibitions throughout the year. The site is a 16th-century timber-framed building
in wonderful Friar Street.

Famous sons of Worcester, where the **Three Choirs Festival** was first held in
1717, include Sir Edward Elgar, born at nearby Broadheath; his statue is a notable landmark opposite the Cathedral.

Finbar and Daryll Ferguson, along with their son Sean, are the tenants of
Drakes Drum, which stands two miles west of Worcester on the 'Elgar Route' -
the composer was born a mile away at Broadheath. The pub is 1950s vintage,
with ample parking and a beer garden with a safe play area that's a popular spot
with families in summer. Inside, it's spacious and open-plan, and customers can
sit wherever they like to enjoy a drink or something to eat. All the food is home-
cooked, and among the top crowd-pleasers are fish & chips cooked in lager
batter, honey-glazed pork and 16oz rump steaks. The daily specials are always a

**Drakes Drum, Tudor Way, St John's, Worcester, Worcestershire WR2 5QL
Tel: 01905 420842**

warm order, and there are dishes for vegetarians; two traditional puddings round things off in style. Banks beer and lagers, good-value wines and spirits. Among other attractions are summer barbecues on the patio and a popular skittle alley.

At the southwestern edge of the city, on the Malvern road, **Bennett's Park Farm**, overlooking the River Teme, is a working farm, open daily in summer, with a museum, farm shop, tea shop and nature trail. Tel: 01905 748102.

AROUND WORCESTER

POWICK   MAP 4 REF G10
2 miles S of Worcester on the A449

Powick Bridge was the scene of the first and last battles in the Civil War; the last, in 1651, ending with Charles hiding in the Boscobel Oak before journeying south to nine year's exile in France. Cromwell's power had been overwhelming, and the long years of strife were at an end. Powick Bridge's skyline is today dominated by Worcester's first power station, built in 1894.

Owners Charles and Maura Ellis and their daughter Tara have extensively renovated the **Red Lion**, a fine old inn on the site of a field hospital for the Battle of Worcester in 1642. Locals and others in the know make a beeline for some of the best pub food in the region, with everything prepared to order from the best raw materials the area can provide. Quick snacks come in the shape of French bread sandwiches and ploughman's platters, while the main menu offers an impressive choice, with great-value steaks always a popular order, along with fish and vegetarian options and the traditional roasts that are the centre-

The Red Lion, Powick, Worcestershire WR2 4QT
Tel: 01905 830203

piece of Sunday lunchtimes. English puddings are the classic way to end a fine meal which could be accompanied by the inn's own-label house wine. Floral displays and hanging baskets add a splash of colour to the exterior, and there's a patio for summer sipping. Inside, the scene is a splendidly old-fashioned one of original beams, porcelain and pictures of the inn's history. The Red Lion has won many awards, including Regional Pub of the Year.

To the east of the city and signposted from the M5 (J6) and from the city centre via the A44, **Worcester Woods Country Park**, open daily, has 50 hectares of ancient oak woodland, 10 hectares of traditional wildflower meadow, waymarked trails, a picnic area, children's play area, visitor centre, café and shop. Tel: 01905 766493.

SPETCHLEY   MAP 4 REF H10
3 miles E of Worcester on the A422

All Saints Church, 14th-century with a 16th-century chapel, is home to a fine collection of monuments to the Berkeley family, who owned adjoining **Spetchley Park**. The park, which extends over 12 hectares, has lovely formal gardens, wooded areas, lawns and a lake with an ornamental bridge.

CROWLE
MAP 4 REF H10

4 miles E of Worcester off the A422

Standing just off the main village street, the Church of St John the Baptist is best known for the strange kneeling figure which faces the congregation from the marble lectern.

HUDDINGTON
MAP 4 REF H9

6 miles E of Worcester on minor roads

Two buildings of particular note: the simple little Church of St James, with a timber-framed bell turret; and **Huddington Court**. The Court has been described as the most picturesque house in Worcestershire. An excellent example of a 16th-century timber-framed building, it was once the home of the Wintours, a staunchly Catholic family who were involved in the Gunpowder Plot. When the plot was exposed and the conspirators finally arrested, both Thomas and Robert Wintour, cousins of Robert Catesby, confessed their guilt and were executed. The Court is a private residence, but you can get a good view of it from the churchyard.

A mile or so north of Huddington lies the village of **Himbleton**, where the Church of St Mary Magdalene has a picturesque bell turret with a memorial clock.

INKBERROW
MAP 4 REF I9

8 miles E of Worcester off the A42

A very pleasant and pretty spot to pause awhile, with the Church of St Peter (note the alabaster of John Savage, a High Sheriff of Worcester who died in 1631), the inn and other buildings round the village green, some in red brick, others black and white half-timbered. The **Old Bull Inn** has two claims to fame, one that William Shakespeare stayed there in 1582, the other that it is the original of The Bull at Ambridge, home of *The Archers*. Photographs of the cast adorn the walls, and the inn has become a place of pilgrimage for fans of the programme.

The Old Vicarage, a handsome 18th-century building in the Tudor style, was host in an earlier guise to King Charles l, who stayed there on his way to Naseby; some maps he left behind are kept in the church.

Ar nearby **Dormston**, a timber-framed **dovecote** stands in front of the Moat farmhouse.

One mile south of Inkberrow is the village of **Abbots Morton**, whose dwellings are mainly 17th-century yeomen's houses. The village was once the site of the Abbot of Evesham's summer residence, but only some mounds and fishponds now remain.

ROUS LENCH
MAP 4 REF I10

1 mile S of Abbots Morton on a minor road

The Lenches are attractive little villages in an area known for its particularly rich soil. Rous Lench church has a chapel with monuments to the Rous family and an oil painting of Jesus in the house of Simon the Pharisee. The road to the hilltop village of **Church Lench** (a mile south), with the church at the very top of the hill, passes by **Rous Lench Court**,the seat of the Rous family for many centuries from 1382. The Court is a splendid half-timbered mansion with a tall Italianate tower in the beautiful gardens.

LOWER BROADHEATH
MAP 4 REF G9

3 miles W of Worcester off the A44

The **Elgar Birthplace Museum** is a redbrick cottage that is crammed with items from the great composer's life. He was born here in 1857 and, despite long periods spent elsewhere, Broadheath remained his spiritual home. The violin was his first instrument, though he eventually succeeded his father as organist at St George's Church in Worcester. He played at the Three Choirs Festival and began conducting locally. He married in 1889 and was soon devoting almost all his time to composing, making his name with *The Enigma Variations* (1899) and *Dream of Gerontius* (1900). He was knighted in 1904 and when in 1931 he was made a baronet by King George V he took the title 1st Baronet of Broadheath. Various Elgar Trails have been established, the one in Worcester city taking in the statue and the *Dream of Gerontius* window in the Cathedral.

LEIGH
MAP 4 REF G10

5 miles W of Worcester off the A4103

The **Church of St Eadburga** is very fine indeed, with some imposing monuments and a marvellous 15th-century rood screen. A curious legend attaches to the church. A man called Edmund Colles is said to have robbed one of his colleagues who was returning from Worcester and known to be carrying a full purse. It was a dark, gloomy night, and as Colles reached out to grab the man's horse, holding on to the bridle, the other struck at him with a sword. When he visited Edmund the next day, the appalling wound testified to the man's guilt; although forgiven by his intended victim, Colles died shortly after and his ghost once haunted the area. A phantom coach pulled by four fire-breathing steeds would appear and race down the hill to the church by Leigh Court, where they would leap over the tithe barn and disappear beneath the waters of the River Teme. A midnight service attended by 12 clergymen eventually laid the ghost to rest. Leaping over the **tithe barn** was no mean feat (though easier of course if you're a ghost), as the 14th-century barn is truly massive, with great cruck beams and porched wagon doors. Standing in the grounds of Leigh Court, a long gabled mansion, the barn is open for visits on summer wekends. Tel: 01743 761101.

Leigh Brook is a tributary of the Teme and wends its way through a spectacular valley cared for by Worcestershire Nature Conservation Trust. The countryside here is lovely, and footpaths make the going easier. Up on Old Storridge Common, birch, ash, oak and bracken have taken a firm hold, and there is a weird, rather unearthly feel about the place. Nearby, the hamlet of **Birch Wood** is where Elgar composed his *Dream of Gerontius*.

ALFRICK
MAP 4 REF G10
7 miles W of Worcester off the A44

Charles Dodgson (Lewis Carroll) once preached at the village Church of St Mary Magdalene, which enjoys a delightful setting above the village green. In the vicinity are two major attractions for nature-lovers. A little way to the northwest is **Ravenshill Woodland Nature Reserve** with waymarked trails through woodland that is home to many breeding birds, while a mile south of Alfrick is the **Knapp and Papermill Nature Reserve**, with 25 hectares of woodland and meadows rich in flora and fauna.

LONGLEY GREEN
MAP 4 REF F10
9 miles W of Worcester off the A44

Two miles south of this, in cider-making country at the foot of the Suckley Hills, is the village of Longley Green. Keep an eye open for **The Nelson Inn**, a traditional village pub set in delightful cider and hop country at the foot of the Suckley Hills. The Worcestershire Way passes close by, so ramblers and walkers often pause for refreshment at this grand old free house, which is run by Graham and Cheryl Harrison and several other members of the family spanning three generations. Refreshment is provided notably by a specialist selection of hand-

The Nelson Inn, Longley Green, Suckley, Worcestershire WR6 5EF
Tel: 01886 884530

pulled cask ales and a wide-ranging menu that includes the 12" Nelson ba-guette, salads and vegetarian dishes, fresh fish on a Friday and the great favourite, steak & kidney pie. Pensioners' lunches Tuesday-Thursday offer particularly good value for money. Book for dinner Thursday to Saturday. Inside, collections of dinner plates and nautical memorabilia take the eye, while outside, Betty's hang-ing baskets are a picture; there are seats outside for 50, and a children's play area. There's a skittles alley where two resident teams play weekly matches. The Nelson, which is open every session except Monday lunchtime, can be reached travelling north from the A4103 or east from the B4214.

BISHOPS FROME   MAP 1 REF F10
12 miles W of Worcester on the B4214

A little way over the border into Herefordshire, in hop country is where the **Hop Pocket Craft Centre** has working kilns and machinery, a craft shop and a restaurant.

Continuing in the traditions of its past, **The Five Bridges**, on the A4103 (Hereford to Worcester road) welcomes travellers for good fayre and fine ales as it has done for centuries. The original building dates back to 1580 but was virtu-ally destroyed in 1645 during the Cromwellian period. It was rebuilt in 1780 and used as a coaching inn and resting place for weary travellers. Mark and Bea Chatterton are the present-day resident proprietors of The Five Bridges and "de-sire that this historic dwelling place provides the very best for all who enter". The mainly home-produced food gives them a good start in their aim of satis-faction. The traditional food is of extremely good quality and well known in the region. Typically, main courses would include: Trout, Steaks, Carbonara, good Vegetarian and children's dishes. But there's a great deal more than that on offer

The Five Bridges, Near Bishops Frome, Worcestershire WR6 5BX
Tel: 01531 640340

and you could start by popping in for coffee and some specially prepared sandwiches to get the rest of the story. Two lounge bars provide plenty of seating area, and once settled in the large, comfortable sofas in front of the lovely old open fire, it's hard to move!

WICHENFORD
Map 4 ref G9

7 miles NW of Worcester on the B4204

A famous landmark here is the National Trust's **Wichenford Dovecote**, a 17th-century timber-framed construction with a lantern on top.

Margaret Nash and her daughter Kate spent two years improving **The Masons Arms**, and the result is a delightful rural stopping place that appeals to a wide variety of visitors. The pub, which lies on the B4204 six miles north-west

Wichenford Dovecote

of Worcester, is a whitewashed 18th century building with comfortable sofas in bright, airy rooms, open log fires in winter and a collection of photographs of

**The Masons Arms, Castle Hill, Wichenford, Worcestershire WR6 6YA
Tel: 01886 888348**

film stars and music greats on the walls. Outside are two large paddocks, a children's play area and an adjacent field where caravaners can park. The new chef offers a comprehensive choice of snacks and full meals, from sandwiches and deep-filled baguettes to cottage pie, chilli con carne, scampi, steaks and Sunday lunchtime roasts. His vegetarian main courses are always in demand. In the summer months, traditional scrumpy cider joins the Banks ales, which are kept in excellent condition. There are lots of scenic walks in the vicinity, plus local fishing and several places of interest including the National Trust's Wichenford Dovecote, a tall 17th century timber-framed dovecote with a lantern on top of its steeply sloping roof.

MARTLEY   MAP 4 REF F9
7 miles NW of Worcester on the B4197

The large village Church of St Peter contains a momument to Hugh Mortimer, who was killed in the Wars of the Roses, and some beautifully preserved wall paintings.

CLIFTON
MAP 4 REF F9

10 miles NW of Worcester on the B4204

In lovely countryside near the River Teme, the village boasts a number of charming dwellings around the green and the Church of St Kenelm. Parts of the church go back to the 12th and 14th centuries.

There are other interesting churches at nearby **Shelsey Beauchamp**, in red sandstone, and **Shelsey Walsh**, with many treasures including the tomb of Sir Francis Walsh. The name of Shelsey Walsh will be familiar to fans of motor sport as the location of a very famous hill climb.

ODDINGLEY
MAP 4 REF H9

5 miles NE of Worcester on minor roads

The parish church of Oddingley stands on a hill overlooking the Worcester & Birmingham Canal. Stained glass is a fine feature.

Walkers, cyclists, motorists and holidaymakers on the neighbouring Worcester-Birmingham Canal join the locals in the **Fir Tree Inn**, which is the life and soul of the tiny hamlet of Dunhampstead in the parish of Oddingley. John and Sue Kearney are the owners of the 200-year-old pub, whose interior features an interesting collection of prints and paintings by a local artist who is also a regular. Their chef seeks out fresh local produce for an à la carte menu of excellent dishes like chicken & ham pie, steak & Guinness pie and rack of lamb with a redcurrant jus. Favourites on the Naughty but Nice puddings board include Spotted Dick, bread & butter pudding, and raspberry pavlova. The Murderer's Bar recalls the grisly events of 1806, when the village parson was shot and then battered to death. The body of the confessed murderer was discovered some 23

**The Fir Tree Inn, Trench Lane, Dunhampstead, Oddingley,
Near Droitwich, Worcestershire WR9 7JX Tel: 01905 774094**

years later and three men were accused of this second murder. They were found guilty but acquitted on a technicality, and one of them, Thomas Clewes, became the landlord here - hence the name of the bar. The pub is open 11-3 and 6-11 Monday to Friday, and all day Saturday and Sunday. One of the rooms is non-smoking. Garden; wheelchair access; baby-changing facilities.

HAWFORD   Map 4 ref G9
4 miles N of Worcester off the A449

Another amazing **dovecote**, this one half-timbered, dating from the 16th century and owned by the National Trust.

DROITWICH   Map 4 ref H9
9 miles N of Worcester on the A38

'Salinae', the place of salt, in Roman times. Salt deposits, a legacy from the time when this area was on the seabed, were mined here for 2,000 years until the end of the 19th century. The natural Droitwich brine contains about 2 1/2 pounds of salt per gallon - ten times as much as sea water - and is often likened to the waters of the Dead Sea. The brine is pumped up from an underground lake which lies 200' below the town. Visitors do not drink the waters at Droitwich as they do at most other spas, but enjoy the therapeutic properties floating in the warm brine. The first brine baths were built in the 1830s and were soon renowned for bringing relief to many and effecting seemingly miraculous cures. By 1876, Droitwich had developed as a fashionable spa, mainly through the efforts of John Corbett, known as the 'Salt King'.

This typical Victorian businessman and philanthropist introduced new methods of extracting the brine and moved the main plant to Stoke Prior. The enterprise was beset with various problems in the 1870s and Corbett turned his attention to developing the town as a spa resort. He was clearly a man of some energy, as he also served as an MP after the 1874 General Election. Many of the buildings in present-day Droitwich were owned by Corbett, including the Raven Hotel (a raven was part of his coat of arms) in the centre. His most remarkable legacy is undoubtedly **Chateau Impney**, on the eastern side of town at Dodderhill. It was designed by a Frenchman, Auguste Tronquois, in the style of an ornate French chateau, with soaring turrets, mansard roof and classical French gardens. It was intended as a home for Corbett and his wife Anna, but she apparently didn't like the place; their increasingly stormy marriage ended in 1884, nine years after the completion of the flamboyant chateau, which is now a high-class hotel and conference centre.

The Heritage and Information Centre (Tel: 01905 774312) includes a local history exhibition (Salt Town to Spa) and a historic BBC radio room.

In the centre of the town is St Andrew's Church, part of whose tower was removed because of subsidence, a condition which affected many buildings and which can be seen in some fairly alarming angles. One of the chapels, dating from the 13th century, is dedicated to St Richard de Wyche, the town's patron saint, who became Bishop of Chichester. On the southern outskirts of Droitwich is the **Church of the Sacred Heart**, built in Italianate style in the 1930s and remarkable for its profusion of beautiful mosaics made from Venetian glass. Many of these mosaics also commemorate the life of St Richard.

One of Droitwich's most famous sons is Edward Winslow, born the eldest of eight children in 1595. He was one of the pilgrims who set sail for the New World to seek religious freedom and he later became Governor of the colony. A bronze memorial to Edward Winslow can be seen in St Peter's Church, Droitwich.

Salwarpe on the southwest fringes of Droitwich, is truly a hidden hamlet, approached by a stone bridge over James Brindley's **Droitwich Canal**. Opened in 1771, the canal linked the town to the River Severn at Hawford. The Church of St Michael, by the edge of the canal, has several monuments to the Talbot family, who owned nearby Salwarpe Court. **Salwarpe Valley Nature Reserve** is one of very few inland sites with salt water, making it ideal for a variety of saltmarsh plants and very well worth a visit.

AROUND DROITWICH

OMBERSLEY   MAP 4 REF G9
3 miles W of Droitwich off the A449

A truly delightful and very English village with some superb black-and-white timbered dwellings with steeply-sloping roofs. St Andrew's Church, rebuilt in 1825, contains memorials to the Sandys family, owners of **Ombersley Court**, a splendid Georgian mansion which can be seen from the churchyard.

HOLT   MAP 4 REF G9
5 miles W of Droitwich off the A443

St Martin's Church is a fine Norman building with an elaborately carved font and several interesting memorials. From outside the church, Holt Castle (not open for visits) can be seen. Just north of Holt, on the A443, is the village of Holt Heath.

Standing proudly alongside the A443, **The Red Lion** is a 350-year-old one-time coaching inn with a patio garden at the back and a children's play area. Smartly redecorated by owners Philomena Hine and Frank Susca, it is open weekdays 12-3.30 and from 5 in the evening, all day at weekends, and attracts plenty of local support as well as passing trade. The comfortable rooms are adorned with a variety of interesting pictures and prints, and one picture in the dining room was presented by Canadian visitors whose grandparents had visited the pub. A full menu is offered, providing hearty portions and great value

**The Red Lion, Witley Road, Holt Heath, Worcestershire WR6 6LX
Tel: 01905 620236**

for money. The list runs from a good range of starters through popular main courses (including vegetarian options) to tempting home-made puddings. Five or six weekly specials add to the choice. The value for money extends to the French house wines, an alternative to their real ales such as Timothy Taylor and London Pride. The River Severn is only a mile away, and there are many interesting places within easy walking distance of this most agreeable pub.

5 North Worcestershire

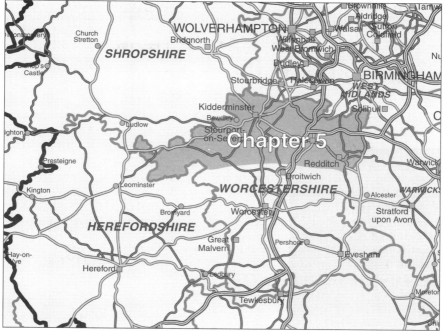

© MAPS IN MINUTES ™ (1998)

Most of Worcestershire's industry was centred in the northern part of the county, and there are numerous examples of industrial archaeology to interest the historian. Salt and scythes, carpets, porcelain and needles all contributed to the local economy, along with ironworks and corn mills, and many fine old buildings survive as monuments to industries which have dwindled or disappeared.

Canals here were once as important as roads, and in this part of the county the Worcester & Birmingham Canal, the Staffordshire & Worcester Canal and the Droitwich Canal were a quicker means of transport than the Severn and more reliable than the roads. They themselves lost a good deal of their practical advantages when the railways arrived. The railway network has shrunk considerably over the last 40 years, so it's back to the roads for most local communications. The Severn Valley Railway, from Kidderminster to Bridgnorth, has survived and flourished, and today people come from far and wide for the chance to ride behind a steam engine through some incredibly beautiful scenery.

Enthusiasts have also ensured that much of the canal system has survived, finding a new role as a major leisure and tourist attraction.

DROITWICH TO BROMSGROVE

The route north from Droitwich towards Bromsgrove takes in much that is of interest to the industrial historian, including the Worcester & Birmingham Canal. Opened in 1815 and 30 miles in length, the canal passes Stoke works ant Stoke Prior, where John Corbett set up his salt works after leaving Droitwich.

BROMSGROVE   Map 4 ref H8
5 miles NE of Droitwich off the A38

A visit to the **Avoncraft Museum of Historic Buildings**, just south of Bromsgrove, is a walk through seven centuries of English history, with each building providing a snapshot of life in its particular period. The first building, a timber-framed merchant's house from Bromsgrove, was brought to the site in 1967, since when over 20 more have been installed. In addition to the buildings themselves, the Museum has regular demonstrations of such crafts as wood-turning, windmilling, racksawing, brick-making, chain-making and nail-making. There's also a shop, refreshment area, picnic site, a children's area, horse-drawn wagon rides and farm animals wandering around freely. One of the most treasured exhibits is the original 14th-century beamed roof of Guesten Hall from Worcester Cathedral, now covering a modern brick building. Tel: 01527 831886. In an area behind the shop is another unique collection, the **BT National Telephone Kiosk Collection**.

Bromsgrove Museum, near the town centre, has displays of local crafts and industry, including the Bromsgrove Guild, an organisation of craftsmen founded in 1894. The Guild of highly skilled craftsmen had its finest hour when commissioned to design and make the gates and railings of Buckingham Palace. Another popular exhibit is a street scene of Victorian shops. Tel: 01527 831809.

Besides the museums, there is plenty to see, including some very handsome timber-framed buildings in the High Street, where stands a statue of AE Housman, the town's most famous son. **Alfred Edward Housman** was born one of seven children at Fockbury, Bromsgrove, in

Bromsgrove Town Crier

1859, and spent his schooldays in the town. After a spell at Oxford University and some time teaching at his old school, he entered the Civil Service in London, where he found time to resume his academic studies. He was appointed Professor of Latin at University College, London, in 1892 and soon afterwards he published his first and best-known collection of poems - *A Shropshire Lad*. His total output was not large, but it includes some of the best-loved poems in the English language. He died in 1936 and is buried in the churchyard of St Lawrence in Ludlow. The forming in 1972 of a Housman Society brought his name to the forefront of public attention and in the region of Bromsgrove walking and driving trails take in the properties and places associated with him.

Bromsgrove has a prestigious annual **music festival** held during the month of May, when the town plays host to a wide range of musical entertainment from orchestral concerts to jazz, and featuring many well-known artists. Another annual event is the revival of the Court Leet, an ancient form of local administration. A colourful procession moves through the town and there's a lively Elizabethan street market.

One of Bromsgrove's old theatres has been converted into a number of retail outlets, one of the stars among them being **Jenny's Jewels & Crafts**. Jenny Gollan opened her shop here in 1997 and has built up an enviable reputation with the

Jenny's Jewels & Crafts, Unit 28-30 1st Floor The Strand Centre, Bromsgrove, Worcestershire B61 8AB Tel: 01527 834979

quality of her products. Everyone who calls in gets the personal touch, from either Jenny herself or her partner Ivy Burley, who is an expert in the fascinating field of dolls' houses. These delightful little houses, along with all the miniature furniture and other accessories, are displayed at one end of the shop. The rest of the shop exhibits crafts across the board, with very reasonable prices to suit all pockets. This was something that Jenny always wanted to do, and her displays show off the tremendous range of mainly local talent. There's costume jewellery, silk flowers, crystalware and a great deal more - a perfect place to look for a special gift. The shop is open 10-4 Mon-Sat and is a must on any visit to Bromsgrove, with something different to delight every time.

The **Church of St John the Baptist** - see his statue over the south porch entrance - contains some superb 19th-century stained glass and an impressive collection of monuments, notably to members of the Talbot family. Side by side in the churchyard are tombs of two railwaymen who were killed in 1840 when their engine exploded while climbing the notorious **Lickey Incline**. This stretch of railway, near the village of **Burcot** three miles northeast of Bromsgrove, is, at 1 in 37.7, the steepest gradient on the whole of the British rail network. One specially powerful locomotive, no. 58100, spent its days up until the late 1950s helping trains up the bank, a task which was later performed by massive double-boilered locomotives that were the most powerful in the then BR fleet. The steepness of the climb is due to the same geographical feature that necessitated the construction of the unique flight of **locks** at **Tardebigge**, between Bromsgrove and Redditch. In the space of 2 1/2 miles the canal is lifted by no fewer than 30 locks. In the actual village of Tardebigge, on the A448, the Church of St Bartholomew enjoys a lovely setting with views across the Severn lowlands.

AROUND BROMSGROVE - SOUTH

HANBURY   MAP 4 REF H9
3 miles S of Bromsgrove off the B4090

Hanbury Hall is a fine redbrick mansion in William & Mary style, completed by Thomas Vernon in 1701. Internal features include murals by Sir James Thornhill, known particularly for his Painted Hall in the Royal Naval Hospital, Greenwich, and frescoes in the dome of St Paul's. See also a splendid collection of porcelain, the Long Gallery, the Moorish gazebos at each corner of the forecourt and the formal gardens with orangery and 18th-century ice house. Tel: 01527 821214.

In beautiful rural surroundings a mile north of the village of Hanbury stands the award-winning **Jinney Ring Craft Centre**. Richard and Jenny Greatwood created this marvellous place by restoring and converting a collection of old timbered barns next to their 17th century farmhouse home. Craftspeople with many diverse skills can be seen at work in their own craft studios, including two

**Jinney Ring Craft Centre, Hanbury, Near Bromsgrove,
Worcestershire B60 4BU Tel: 01527 821272**

potters, a violin-maker, a jeweller, a picture-framer, a leatherworker, a sign-maker
and an antiques restorer. Also on the premises is a craft gallery with changing
exhibitions by British craftsmen and artists, and a clothes and knitwear department. There is always a wide variety of items for sale. Morning coffee, lunch and
afternoon tea are served in the farmhouse kitchen, which enjoys lovely views
over duck ponds towards the Malvern Hills. A visit here is both a joy and an
education, and visitors eager to learn even more can enrol in a one-day or two-
day course which the centre holds and which cover upwards of 60 different
skills.

REDDITCH   MAP 4 REF I9
6 miles SE of Bromsgrove on the A448

A 'New Town' from the 60s, but there is plenty of history here, as well as some
great walking. The **Arrow Valley Country Park**, a few minutes walk from the
town centre, comprises a vast expanse of parkland with nature trails, picnic areas
and lovely walks. Sailing, canoeing, windsurfing and fishing are popular pas-
times on the lake.

Housed in historic buildings in the beautiful Arrow Valley, **Forge Mill Needle
Museum & Bordesley Abbey Visitor Centre** offers a unique glimpse into a past
way of life. The Needle Museum threads its way through the fascinating history

Forge Mill Needle Museum & Bordesley Abbey Visitor Centre, Needle Mill Lane, Riverside, Redditch, Worcestershire B98 8HY Tel: 01527 62509

of the Redditch needle-making industry, with the original water-powered machinery and re-created scenes showing vividly how needles were made in the 19th century. The link with needles has established the museum as a leading centre for textile-lovers, with exhibitions, workshops and a shop selling unusual needles and sewing accessories. A major annual event is the Charles Henry Foyle Trust-sponsored national needlework competition, and other events for 1999 include a show of antique Welsh quilts and the Forge Mill embroidery group (24 April-27 June). The tea room is open during some of the events. A short walk brings visitors to the ruins of Bordesley Abbey, a medieval Cistercian abbey where archaeological finds are on display and a new archaeological activity centre can be booked for special events. Send for a leaflet for a full list of the events at these two very special places, both run by Redditch Borough Council. Open daily except Friday and Saturday in winter.

ASTWOOD BANK
Map 4 ref I9
4 miles S of Redditch on the A441

Many attractions both inside and out at **The White Lion**, which stands by the A441 a few miles south of Redditch. A Grade ll Listed building, full of old-world charm and mystery (the haunting stories are legion), it was once a coaching inn and is the oldest public house in the area. The tenants are Paul and Joanna Bennell, delightful people with a warm welcome for the whole family. Food is served

**The White Lion, Astwood Bank, Worcestershire B96 6AA
Tel: 01527 892504**

every session except Sunday, and to accompany it are well-kept ales (Banks Bitter, Mild, Smoothpour) and Weston's traditional scrumpy. The pub holds a children's licence, and the little ones are really well looked after: they have their own special menu, and in the huge, leafy garden they can romp in a super play area, with bark chippings under the various activities to guarantee a soft landing. Live music is laid on once a week (either Friday or Saturday) in a large function room, and on Sunday night a quiz gets under way at 9 o'clock.

FECKENHAM   MAP 4 REF I9
4 miles S of Redditch on the B4090

A pretty village with half-timbered, redbrick and Georgian houses and the fine Church of St John the Baptist. Inside the church a board displays the benefaction which Charles l bestowed upon the village in 1665 - £6, 13 shillings and fourpence, payable out of forest land to the school. The forest in question once surrounded the village, but the trees were all felled for fuelling the saltpans and no trace of the forest now remains.

In this picturesque village stands **The Rose & Crown**, a lovely old pub with a long and fascinating history. After running a hotel for many years, Paddy and Thereze McWalter bought the pub back in 1983 and now have the assistance of their five children. Blazing fires add to the warm, inviting atmosphere in this splendid hostelry, which has a separate restaurant with 45 covers and silver service - an ideal place for a special occasion, but booking is necessary at any time. All the family take a hand in the kitchen, so this is absolutely guaranteed,

**The Rose & Crown, 48 High Street, Feckenham, Near Redditch,
Worcestershire B96 6HS Tel: 01527 892188**

genuine home cooking. The menu is full of interest with such dishes as mussels cooked with white wine, shallots and cream, chicken and herb raviolo, poached salmon with a butter sauce, venison steak in red wine, and chargrilled lamb steak with a cranberry and port wine sauce. Complementing the excellent food is a good choice of beer and cider. The Rose & Crown is so close to the parish church that it must have played a major part in church life. It is probably approaching 500 years old, and its name is shared by many alehouses that were renamed at the end of the War of the Roses in 1485. The ghost that is part of this particular pub's romantic history has not been seen since the McWalters arrived. Perhaps there's no room for him! The pub is open every session and all day Saturday and Sunday, but no food is served on Sunday evenings. Live music on the last Sunday in the month.

WYTHALL

MAP 4 REF I8

6 miles N of Redditch on the A435

Right on the other side of Redditch, and well on the way to Birmingham, is the **Birmingham and Midland Museum of Transport**. Founded in 1977, the Museum's two large halls house a marvellous collection of some 100 buses and coaches, battery vehicles and fire engines, many having seen service in Birmingham and the West Midlands. Open Saturday and Sunday in summer. Tel: 01564 826471.

AROUND BROMSGROVE - NORTH

5 miles north of Bromsgrove lies **Wasely Hill** where open hillside and woodland offers great walking and spectacular views from the top of Windmill Hill. There is also a visitor centre. Just to the east there is more great walking and views in a varied landscape around the **Lickey Hills** which also has a visitor centre.

BELBROUGHTON   MAP 4 REF H8
6 miles N of Bromsgrove on the B4188

This village was once a centre of the scythe-making industry. Holy Trinity Church occupies a hillside site along with some pleasing Georgian buildings.

A little to the north are the village of **Clent** and the **Clent Hills**, an immensely popular place for walking and drinking in the views. On the top are four large upright stones which could be statement-making modern art but for the fact that they were put there over 200 years ago by Lord Lyttleton of Hagley Hall. Walton Hill is over 1,000 feet above sea level.

HAGLEY   MAP 4 REF H7
8 miles N of Bromsgrove off the A491

George, 1st Lord Lyttleton, commissioned, in 1756, the creation of what was to be the last great Palladian mansion in Britain, **Hagley Hall**. Imposing without, exotic and rococo within; notable are the Barrell Room with panelling from Holbeach Hall, where two of the Gunpowder Plotters - the Wintour brothers - were caught and later put to death in the favourite way of hanging, drawing and quartering. Temples, cascading pools and a ruined castle are some of the reasons for lingering in the park, which has a large herd of deer. Tel: 01562 882408.

Another attraction at Hagley is the **Falconry Centre** (Tel: 01562 700014) on the A4565, where owls, hawks, falcons and eagles live and fly.

BROMSGROVE TO KIDDERMINSTER

Not far out of Bromsgrove, north of the A448, lies the village of **Dodford**, whose Church of the Holy Trinity and St Mary is an outstanding example of an Arts and Crafts church, designed by the Bromsgrove in 1908.

CHADDESLEY CORBETT   MAP 4 REF H8
4 miles W of Bromsgrove on the A448

A fairly sizeable village, dominated at its southern end by the 14th-centruy Church of St Cassian. It is the only church in England to be dedicated to this saint, who was born in Alexandria in the 5th century and became a bishop in Africa. He was also a schoolmaster and was apparently killed by his pupils.

Local residents, motorists, cyclists and ramblers are united in their praise of the hospitality and good cheer at **The Swan Inn**, which stands on the main street through a pretty village of half-timbered dwellings, with a church that's well worth a visit and nearby woods to explore. New managers Shaun and Sarah

The Swan Inn, The Village, Chaddesley Corbett, Near Bromsgrove, Worcestershire DY10 4SD Tel: 01562 777302

McKeown offer an imaginative selection of home-cooked meals, including barbecues when the weather's fine, a very popular mixed grill and always a choice of vegetarian dishes. Top-condition real ales include the prize-winning Batham's Black Country. The white-painted inn dates back as far as the early part of the 16th century, when it started life as a coaching inn, and the lofty lounge was once the barn where the stages unloaded their passengers. The 26-cover restaurant is a non-smoking area. Children are welcome, and they have a play area in the lovely garden.

HARVINGTON

MAP 4 REF H8

5 miles W of Bromsgrove near junction of A448/A450

Harvington Hall is a moated medieval and Elizabethan manor house with a veritable maze of rooms. Mass was celebrated here during times when it was a very dangerous thing to do, and that is perhaps why the Hall has more priest holes than any other house in the land. Tel: 01562 777846.

HARTLEBURY

MAP 4 REF G8

3 miles S of Kidderminster off the A449

Hartlebury Castle, a historic sandstone castle of the Bishops of Worcester and a prison for captured Royalist troops in the Civil War, now houses the **Worcester County Museum** (Tel: 01299 250416). In the former servants' quarters in the north wing numerous permanent exhibitions show the past lives of the county's

Hatlebury Castle

inhabitants from Roman times to the 20th century. Visitors can also admire the grandeur of the three Castle State Rooms.

Lynne Knight runs a very special B&B establishment located in one of several hamlets on the A449 between Ombersley and Hartlebury. Her **Yew Tree House** is a Georgian building, and the five letting bedrooms (all en suite) are individually decorated with style and taste. Three rooms are in the main house, while the two

Yew Tree House, Norchard, Crossway Green, Near Hartlebury,
Worcestershire DY13 9SN Tel: 01299 250921 Mobile: 0403 112 392

new rooms are in an adjacent half-timbered cottage. The lounge is a lovely room with a log fire, antiques and Victorian watercolours. A full English or Continental breakfast is served, with evening meals by arrangement. Guests may use the honesty bar for a glass of wine or spirits. A great feature here is the secluded garden, where over 100 types of rose are grown. A tennis court is available for guests' use, and Ombersley golf club is a very short drive away.

On Hartlebury Common, **Leapgate Country Park** is a nature reserve in heath and woodland, with the county's only acid bog.

KIDDERMINSTER
MAP 4 REF G8
9 miles NW of Bromsrove on the A448

Known chiefly as a centre of the carpet-making industry, which began here early in the 18th century as a cottage industry. The introduction of the power loom brought wealth to the area and instigated the building of carpet mills. Standing on the River Stour, the town has a variety of mills, whose enormous chimneys dominate the skyline and serve as architectural monuments to Kidderminster's heritage. St Mary's Church, on a hill overlooking the town, is the largest parish church in the county and contains some superb tomb monuments. The Whittall Chapel, designed in 1922 by Sir Charles Gilbert Scott, was paid for by Matthew Whittall, a native of Kidderminster who went to America and made a fortune in carpets. Three beautiful windows depicting the Virgin Mary, Joan of Arc and

Florence Nightingale, were given by his widow in his memory. Kidderminster's best-known son is Rowland Hill, who founded the modern postal system and introduced the penny post; he was also a teacher, educationalist and inventor. His statue stands outside the Town Hall. By the station on the Severn Valley Railway is the **Kidderminster Railway Museum** (Tel: 01562 825316) with a splendid collection of railway memorabilia. Run by volunteers, it is housed in an old GWR grain store.

Just outside town, at **Stone**, on the A448, is Stone House Cottage Garden, a lovely walled garden with towers. Unusual wall shrubs, climbers and herbaceous plants are featured, most of them for sale in the nursery. Tel: 01562 69902.

In the Stour Valley just north of Kidderminster is the village of **Wolverley**, with charming cottages and pretty gardens, the massive Church of St John the Baptist, and the remains - not easy to see - of prehistoric cave dwellings in the red sandstone cliffs.

Statue of Rowland Hill, Kidderminster

AROUND KIDDERMINSTER

SHATTERFORD   MAP 4 REF G7
2 miles N of Kidderminster on the A442

Shatterford Wildlife Sanctuary (Tel: 01299 861597) is home to Sika deer, red deer, goats, sheep, wild boar, pot-bellied pigs and koi carp.

Two miles further north, off the A442, **Kingsford Country Park** covers 200 acres of heath and woodland that is home to a wide variety of birdlife. It extends into Kinver Edge, across the border into Staffordshire, and many waymarked walks start at this point.

BEWDLEY   MAP 4 REF G8
3 miles W of Kidderminster on the A456

On the western bank of the Severn, linked to its suburb Wribbenhall by a fine Thomas Telford Bridge, Bewdley was once a flourishing port, but lost some of its importance when the Staffordshire & Worcestershire Canal was built. It's a quiet, civilised but much visited little town with some good examples of Georgian

Severn Valley Railway

architecture, and has won fame with another form of transport, the **Severn Valley Railway**.

Guaranteed to excite young and old alike, the **Severn Valley Railway** operates a full service of timetabled trains hauled by a variety of steam locomotives. The service runs from Kidderminster to Bridgnorth, home of the railway since 1965, and the route takes in such scenic attractions as the Wyre Forest and the Severn Valley Country Park and Nature Reserve. Each of the six stations is an architectural delight, and there are buffets at Bridgnorth and Kidderminster, and a tea room at Bewdley. One of the most popular offerings is Sunday lunch on the move, with trains starting from both Bridgnorth and Kidderminster. Advance booking for dining is essential: call 01299 403816. The same number gets through to the booking service for the footplate experience courses, where railway buffs and children (current or second time round) can realise a dream by learning to fire and drive a steam locomotive. Special events take place throughout the year,

Severn Valley Railway, The Railway Station, Bewdley, Worcestershire DY12 1BG Tel: 01299 403816 http://www.svr.co.uk

and in 1999 they include Thomas the Tank Engine weekends (May 15/16 & 22/23), a nostalgic 1940s weekend (July 3/4), an autumn steam gala (September 24-26) and a classic vehicle day on October 10. In Kidderminster itself additional attractions include a railway museum and the King & Castle public house serving an excellent choice of home-cooked food and real ales.

Bewdley Museum, which also incorporates the Tourist Information Centre, is a great place for all the family, with exhibitions themed around the River Severn and the **Wyre Forest**. Crafts depicted include charcoal-burning, coopering and brass-making. Bewdley was the birthplace of Stanley Baldwin, three times Prime Minister between the Wars.

CALLOW HILL
MAP 4 REF F8

2 miles W of Bewdley on the A456

The **Wyre Forest Visitor Centre** (Tel: 01299 266944) is set among mature oak woodland with forest walks, picnic area, gift shop and restaurant. Wyre Forest covers a vast area starting northwest of Bewdley and extending into Shropshire. The woodland, home to abundant flora and fauna, is quite dense in places. It was once inhabited by nomadic people who made their living from what was around them, weaving baskets and brooms, burning charcoal and making the little wooden whisks which were used in the carpet-making process. Just south of Callow Hill, the village of **Rock** has an imposing Norman church in a prominent hillside position with some lovely windows and carving.

The Duke William public house stands on the main A456 road at Callow Hill, a mile or so west of Bewdley at the southern edge of the majestic 600-acre Wyre Forest. Julie Baker, having spent many years as a bookkeeper, took the plunge into the licensed trade and became the tenant here in November 1998,

The Duke William, Callow Hill, Rock, Near Bewdley, Worcestershire DY14 9XH Tel: 01299 266012

making an immediate impression. The locals really appreciate her warm, friendly personality, and one of the regulars swears that the beer even tastes better since her arrival! Real fires add to the inviting feel. The food is a major attraction, served every day except Sunday night and Monday, and the varied menu, boosted by a specials board, always includes a generous choice for vegetarians. Sunday lunch with roast beef, pork, lamb and chicken is a particularly popular occasion. The building itself is difficult to date, but it probably became a public house in the middle of the 19th century. It once had stabling and a smithy. A fine pub going places under an enthusiastic and very likeable tenant.

STOURPORT-ON-SEVERN   MAP 4 REF G8
2 miles S of Bewdley on the A451

At the centre of the Worcestershire waterways is the unique Georgian 'canal town' of Stourport, famous for its intricate network on canal basins. There was not much trade, nor even much of a town, before the canals came, but prosperity came quickly once the **Staffordshire & Worcestershire Canal** had been dug. The commercial trade has gone, but the town still prospers, the barges laden with

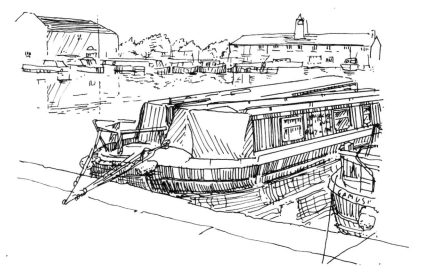

Canal Basin, Stourport-on-Severn

coal, timber, iron and grain having given way to pleasure craft. Many of the old barges have been renovated and adapted to this new role.

The lovely old **Bridge Inn** is situated 100 yards from the River Severn in popular, picturesque Stourport. The pub goes back to the 1770s and once had stabling not only for coach horses but also for the horses that towed barges along

The Bridge Inn, 10 Bridge Street, Stourport-on-Severn, Worcestershire DY13 8UX Tel: 01299 877475

the canals. You can sit anywhere to enjoy a meal, with the flagstoned conservatory overlooking the gardens a non-smoking area, along with parts of the main dining section. The bar has a fishing theme, with old baskets, nets and assorted bits and pieces. The menu runs from filled baguettes and jacket potatoes to burgers, pies, monster mixed grills, jumbo cod & chips and the daily chef's specials. David and Jane Woodhead are the licensees, and since they arrived in April 1998 the pub has become known for its exceptional ales - David had more than 60 guest ales in his first few months alone and has been selected for inclusion in CAMRA's Good Beer Guide. Hanging baskets and garden tubs produce a blaze of colour in the summer, when the pub is open all day, with food served lunchtime and evening; in winter, food is served lunchtime every day except Monday and evenings Wednesday to Saturday. Children welcome. Wheelchair access. Quiz night Tuesday; live music alternate Thursdays.

Naomi Hill and her father David have put their business and catering skills to excellent use in **The Old Anchor Inn**, situated on the southern edge of town near the River Stour and the canal basin. Behind its neat exterior, this free house offers Victorian-style looks and comfort, with deep, inviting sofas and wood panelling. At night, the pretty lounge-restaurant twinkles with candlelight. Bar

**The Old Anchor Inn, Worcester Road, Stourport-on-Severn,
Worcestershire DY13 9AR Tel: 01299 822655**

customers can enjoy pool in the games room as well as excellent beers. Naomi, who has a hotel and catering degree, offers a menu to suit all appetites, with an extensive choice of wines. Mouthwatering foreign dishes and fresh fish often feature as chef's specials too. Sunday lunches topped off with delicious traditional puddings are a firm local favourite, and jazz fans can enjoy live music every month. A children's licence means families can stay until 9.30pm as well as enjoy the pretty garden in the summer.

ASTLEY   MAP 4 REF G8
3 miles S of Stourport on the A451

Stanley Baldwin (1867-1947) died at Astley Hall, opposite which, by the B4196, stands a memorial stone inscribed "Thrice Prime Minister". Astley is also home to **Astley Vineyards** (Tel: 01299 822907), a working vineyard producing award-winning white wines, with a vineyard trail and a shop. Go by car, by bus - or by boat, as they have mooring facilities.

ABBERLEY   MAP 4 REF F8
4 miles SW of Stourport off the A451

A truly delightful little place, surrounded by hills. The Norman Church of St Michael was saved from complete dilapidation in the 1960s, and the part that survives, the chancel, is certainly well worth a visit, not only for its charming ambience but also for the treasures it holds. On the other side of the hill is Abberley Hall, now a school, with a Big Ben-like bell tower that can be seen for miles around. Old Boys include Geoffrey Howe.

GREAT WITLEY
MAP 4 REF F9
5 miles SW of Stourport on the A443

There are two great reasons not to miss this place! **Great Witley Church**, almost ordinary from the outside, has an unbelievable interior of Baroque flamboyance that glows with light in a stunning ambience of gold and white. Masters of their crafts contributed to the interior, which was actually removed from the Chapel of Canons in Edgware: Joshua Price stained glass, Bellucci ceiling paintings, Bagutti plasterwork. Next to the church are the spectacular and hauntingly beautiful remains of **Witley Court**, a palatial mansion funded by the riches of the Dudley family. Destroyed by fire in 1937, it stood a neglected shell for years, until English Heritage took over these most splendid of ruins and started the enormous task of making them safe and accessible. If you only see one ruin in the whole county, this should be it. Tel: 01299 896636

Visitors come from far and wide to appreciate the unique charms of **Home Farm**, which enjoys a lovely setting at the foot of the Abberley Hills. Anne and Roger Kendrick offer splendid bed and breakfast accommodation in four spacious bedrooms with tasteful furnishings and original beams. One has a bathroom en suite, the others share a separate shower room. The house itself, a Grade ll* listed building, was once part of the Witley Court estate, built by the Foley family of ironmasters and industrial developers. Delightful gardens surround the house, and a pond complete with resident ducks adds to the peaceful, serene atmos-

**Home Farm, Great Witley, Worcestershire, WR6 6JJ. Tel: 01299 896825
Fax: 01299 896176**

phere. Guests have their own sitting room with satellite TV. A choice of breakfasts is available, with local produce always to the fore. No smoking, no dogs and - because of the water - no children under 10. The area offers some wonderful walks, and a visit to the parish church, with its unique Baroque interior, is a must.

TENBURY WELLS   MAP 1 REF E8
9 miles SW of Bewdley on the A456

The A443 leads from Great Witley towards Shropshire and the border town of Tenbury Wells in a delightfully rural setting on the River Teme. The 'Wells' was added when a source of mineral water was discovered, but its heyday as a spa resort was very brief. **Tenbury Museum** (Tel: 01584 811669) tells the spa story and depicts other aspects of local life, including hop-growing and the railway days.

Dermot Aherne is the new owner of **The Wine Vaults**, a splendid little pub that is easy to miss in the town centre near the recently renovated Spa Rooms. It's a big favourite among local residents, and fund-raising for charity is a major activity. It's a wet pub, with only nibbles to accompany the beers and the local farmhouse cider. Tenbury Wells is famous for its hops, attracting pickers from all over the country, and a wooden casing of hops and grapes makes an unusual decoration on the ceiling of the bar. Tenbury is also a magnet for fishermen (it stands on the River Teme) but never quite made it as a spa town, although mineral waters were discovered in 1839. But it's an excellent place for browsing around the shops - and dropping in at this super little pub!

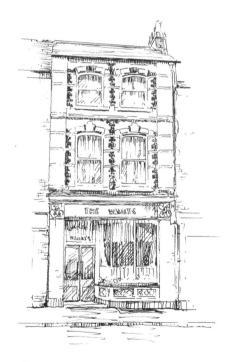

Set in sweeping lawns on the banks of the Teme, in the village of **Burford** a mile west of Tenbury (and just in Shropshire) stands **Burford House**, whose four-acre gardens are filled with well over 2,000 varieties of plants. This is the home of the National Collection of

The Wine Vaults, Teme Street, Tenbury Wells, Worcestershire WR15 8BB Tel: 01584 811883

Clematis, and in the nursery attached to the garden almost 400 varieties of clematis are for sale, along with many other plants and gifts. The ground floor of the house is open as a gallery of contemporary art. Teas and light meals are served in the Burford Buttery. Tel: 01584 810777.

The trip through Worcestershire ends at this point, with just a scent of the delights that wait across the border in Shropshire.

6 South Shropshire

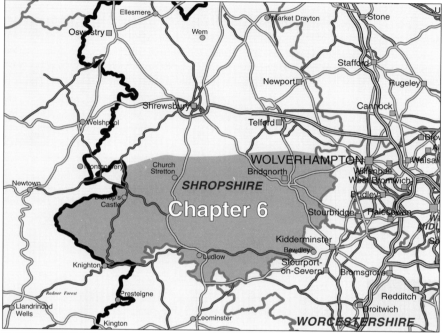

© MAPS IN MINUTES ™ (1998)

Out of Worcestershire and into Shropshire, recently accorded the title of *"The Most Romantic County in Britain"*. A tranquil face hides an often turbulent past that is revealed at scores of sites by the remains of dykes and ramparts and hill forts, and by the castles of the Marcher Lords, who seem to have divided their time between fighting the Welsh and fighting each other. The county boasts some of Britain's most important Roman sites, notably at Wroxeter, which at one time was the fourth largest Roman town in the land. Shropshire beckons with a landscape of great variety: the little hills and valleys, the lakes and canals of the northwest, the amazing parallel hill ranges towards the south, the rich farming plains around Oswestry, the forests of Clun and Wyre, Ironbridge Gorge, called "the birthplace of the Industrial Revolution". Add to this the historic towns of Shrewsbury, Ludlow and Oswestry, the churches and the stately homes and the glorious gardens and you have a part of the world just waiting to be explored, whether by car, on a bike or on foot. South Shropshire affords a trip through romance and history, including the wonderful town of Ludlow and the spectacular scenery of Wenlock Ridge, Long Mynd and Clun Forest.

CLEOBURY MORTIMER

Map 3 ref F8

5 miles W of Bewdley on the A4117

A famous landmark at Cleobury Mortimer is the crooked spire of **St Mary's Church**, whose east window commemorates William Langland. His best known work is *Piers Plowman*. It was in this village that Maisie Bloomer, a witch, gained notoriety in the 18th century. Curses and love potions were her speciality, and the villagers were in no doubt that she was in league with the Devil.

The High Street, Cleobury Mortimer

The only pub in the country to be called **The Blount Arms** is named after Sir Walter Blount and was built in 1863. The inside is absolutely charming, and excellent hospitality is offered by Robert and Eileen Bagley, who took over as owners in 1996. Eileen is in charge of food, which she provides in abundance

The Blount Arms, Forest Park, Cleobury Mortimer, Near Kidderminster, Shropshire DY14 9BE Tel: 01299 270423

and at very affordable prices to an appreciative band of regulars and visitors. The good fare is complemented by a fine selection of ales, including varieties from Banks and Hobsons. On a nearby stretch of disused railway line the owners have created a secluded caravan/camping site with good standings and facilities including electric hook-ups - a handy base for touring this lovely part of the country, which is also popular with walkers and cyclists. The pub, which stands alongside the A4117, is not open until 4 o'clock on Mondays in winter; food is not served on Sunday evenings.

Two miles east of Cleobury stands **Mawley Hall**, an 18th-century stone house with some very fine internal features.

CLEE HILL   MAP 2 REF E8
5 miles W of Cleobury Mortimer on the A4117

The Clee Hills to the north of the village include the highest peaks in the county. The summit of **Brown Clee** is 1750' above sea level.

The Royal Oak stands on the A4117 surrounded by beautiful countryside. Equally easy on the eye, with an immaculate whitewashed exterior, the pub, which dates from the middle of the 18th century, was a coaching inn with stabling - very necessary to provide relief teams of horses after the arduous climb up Clee Hill. Kevin Mooney is the owner and chef, and his efforts and

The Royal Oak, Angel Bank, Clee Hill, Near Ludlow, Shropshire SY8 3PE
Tel: 01584 890485

expertise have turned the Royal Oak into a real winner with both locals and outsiders. All the familiar favourites appear on his quality menus, which include dishes from Italy and the Orient, and a separate omelette menu. There's also a grill menu, on which the Stegosaurus Grill, with rump steak, pork chop, Barnsley chop, gammon steak, sausages, eggs, tomatoes and mushrooms is strictly only for trenchermen! Excellent ales are on tap to accompany the fine food or to enjoy by themselves. Food is served 12-7 Monday-Thursday (later by booking), 12-10 Friday & Saturday and 12-3 on Sunday. Friday night is karaoke night, with a DJ in the function room and a late-night licence. Next to the pub is a large field where visitors can put up a tent or park their caravan.

LUDLOW

MAP 2 REF D8

12 miles NW of Cleobury Mortimer on the A49

Often called 'the perfect historic town', Ludlow has more than 500 listed buildings, and the medieval street pattern has been kept virtually intact. **Ludlow Castle** was built by the Normans in the 11th century, one of a line of castles along the Marches to keep out the Welsh. Under its protection a large town was planned and built - and prospered, due to the collection and sale of wool and the manufacture of cloth. The Castle has been home to many distinguished families and to Royalty: Edward V, Prince Arthur and other Royal children were brought up in Ludlow, and the Castle became the headquarters of the Council of the Marches, which governed Wales and the border counties until 1689. Nowadays the past combines dramatically with the future in the **Holodeck**, where hologram images create ultra-realistic 3D illusions. The Giant Kaleidoscope gives the viewer the sensation of standing before a globe of light and an ever-chang-

Ludlow Castle

ing surface of colours, and the **Well of Infinity** is an apparently bottomless hole in the ground - on the first floor. Tel: 01584 873355.

Overlooking Ludlow Castle in the heart of south Shropshire, **The Cliffe Hotel** is an ideal place for exploring the area's rich variety of scenery and history, or just to get away for a well-earned break. Built in 1867 and standing in its own extensive grounds, the hotel has nine well-equipped bedrooms including singles, doubles, twins and family rooms, all with en suite facilities and central heating. Owners Roger and Helen Jones came here in 1997 after long careers in teaching, and Helen keeps guests happy with her excellent cooking. There are separate menus for bar and restaurant, the former embracing sandwiches, grills, vegetarian dishes and old favourites like roast chicken and steak & kidney pie. The evening menu (best to book for a table in the restaurant) adds variety to these classics with daily specials such as prawn fritters with a spicy dip or mushroom and chestnut parcel with stout and stilton. There's always a tempting

The Cliffe Hotel, Dinham, Ludlow, Shropshire SY8 2JE
Tel: 01584 872063 Fax: 01584 873991

array of sweets to round things off in style. Non-residents are welcome, even if it's just for a drink. No smoking except at the bar.

During its 250-year history **The George** has played a variety of roles, becoming a public house at the end of the 19th century. Since taking over early in 1998 Sharon Griffiths has breathed new life into the place, providing a cheerful rendezvous in the historic centre of Ludlow where regulars and casual visitors mix happily in an atmosphere that bustles from opening time to last orders. Good-quality ales are dispensed from gleaming brass taps in the bar, and throughout the day and into the evening an extensive choice of snacks and full meals is available: baguettes with interesting fillings such as hot pork with stuffing and gravy, burgers, picnic and ploughman's platters, omelettes, Thai-style fishcakes, gammon steaks with all the trimmings; a traditional roast is served Sunday lunchtime. Sharon is particularly proud of the pub's patio beer garden, which she created to

The George, Castle Square, Ludlow, Shropshire SY8 1AT. Tel: 01584 872055

provide an alfresco setting for enjoying a drink or a meal. The George also boasts a night club, above the main bar area, which is open Friday and Saturday evenings for over-18s.

The parish church of St Laurence is one of the largest in the county, reflecting the town's affluence at the time of its rebuilding in the 15th century. There are fine misericords and stained glass, and the poet AE Housman, author of "*A Shropshire Lad*", is commemorated in the churchyard. Other places which should be seen include **Castle Lodge**, once a prison and later home of the officials of the Council of the Marches, and the fascinating houses that line Broad Street.

The historic Corve district of Ludlow is liberally scattered with buildings going back to the 17th century, but few are more impressive than **The Unicorn Inn**. Full of character and old-world charm, the inn has a part-timbered exterior, beamed ceilings and a roaring log fire in winter. In the capable hands of the Ditchburn family (Alan and Elisabeth, son Jon and daughter Helen), this very

The Unicorn Inn, Lower Corve Street, Ludlow, Shropshire SY8 1DU
Tel: 01584 873555

special free house is open lunchtime and evening every day, and visitors can be assured of a cheerful welcome, good food in the restaurant and a pleasant drink (well-kept real ales) in the panelled bar. There are two dining areas, with 75 seats in total, and it's best to book on Friday and Saturday evenings. There's a choice of à la carte and fixed-price menus, with the main emphasis on classic English cuisine. Typical dishes run from chicken liver paté and whitebait among the starters to super main courses such as pork tenderloin with a cider and mustard sauce, or salmon with a pink peppercorn sauce. Nut roast and locally produced meatless sausages cater for vegetarians, and home-made desserts or ice cream round off the meal in style. The inn has one letting bedroom, a very cosy double with bathroom en suite.

Ludlow Museum, in Castle Street (Tel: 01584 873857), has exhibitions of local history centred on, among other things, the Castle, the town's trade and special features on local geology and archaeology. **The Ludlow Festival**, held annually since 1960 and lasting a fortnight in June/July, has become one of the major arts festivals in the country. The centrepiece of the festival, an open-air performance of a Shakespeare play in the Castle's inner bailey, is supported by a number of events that have included orchestral concerts, musical recitals, literary and historical lectures, exhibitions, readings and workshops. At one time in the last century glove-making was one of the chief occupations in the town. Nine master glovers employed some 700 women and children, each required to produce ten pairs of gloves a week, mainly for the American market.

Historians will have to dig deep to uncover the full story of **Ye Olde Bull Ring Tavern**, which has few rivals when it comes to period style and character. A hostelry has stood on this site since 1365 and the present facade, with its

Ye Olde Bull Ring Tavern, 44 The Bull Ring, Ludlow, Shropshire SY8 1AB
Tel: 01584 872311

elaborate half-timbering and honeycomb windows, dates from the middle of the 17th century. The place was closed for six months before June and Gary Merrill took over in early 1999, and the major refurbishment has served to enhance the enormous charm of the beams, panelling and uneven floors that characterise the interior. This is very much a place to come for a leisurely meal, and the main menu is available in the eyecatching first-floor restaurant during long lunchtime and evening sessions Monday to Saturday and from noon to 4.30 on Sunday. Steaks are a popular order, served with a choice of sauces, and there are always several fishy main courses and a vegetarian dish of the day. Waitress service, children welcome. Behind this most atmospheric of taverns is a secluded beer garden.

AROUND LUDLOW

WOOFFERTON

MAP 1 REF D8

4 miles S of Ludlow at A49/A456 junction

Excellent cooking is a major feather in the cap of **The Salwey Arms**, a fine Georgian building standing by the A49 where it meets the A456 a few miles south of Ludlow. Christine and Stephen Rees, here for three years but in the trade for 20, propose restaurant and bar menus that are both long on variety and high on quality, and daily blackboard specials provide even more choice. Classics such as steaks and lasagne are joined by less usual dishes such as

The Salwey Arms, Woofferton, Near Ludlow, Shropshire SY8 4AL
Tel: 01584 711203 Fax: 01584 711159

chargrilled Cajun salmon with cucumber and mint raita, or medallions of pork glazed with Applewood smoked cheese served on a tian of sweet potatoes and sage stuffing. A particular favourite is the Salwey combo of marinated chicken, pork spare rib chop, spiced potato wedges and Cajun mushrooms. Booking is recommended at peak eating times and weekends. An old range is a decorative feature in the dining area, while in the bar hang tools and implements of yester-year. Well-kept ales, including some local brews, and a well-chosen wine list provide a fine accompaniment to the food. The cooking is not the only attraction here, as top-notch overnight accommodation is available in three letting bedrooms with showers and washbasins.

MIDDLETON

MAP 2 REF E8

2 miles NE of Ludlow on the B4364

Bernadette and Tom Chivers welcome guests to **The Moor Hall**, a handsome house built in 1789 in Georgian Palladian style. The setting, in five acres of gardens and woodland, is one of great beauty and serenity, with breathtaking views over miles of unspoilt countryside, and the atmosphere is totally relaxed.

The Moor Hall, Near Ludlow, Shropshire SY8 3EG
Tel: 01584 823209 Fax: 01584 823387

The gardens provide a perfect opportunity for a leisurely stroll, while the hills and valleys beyond beckon the more energetic visitor. The three en suite bedrooms (no smoking) combine all the modern comforts with the traditional qualities of the English country house lifestyle; like the rest of this beautifully kept house, they are decorated and furnished with impeccable taste. Evening meals are available, and most guests take them, as Bernadette is a very fine cook. This most civilised place stands on the B4364, 2 ½ miles east of the village of Middleton on the road to Bridgnorth, and only four miles from Ludlow.

BROMFIELD
MAP 2 REF D8
3 miles NW of Ludlow on the A49

St Mary's Church is noted for its exotic interior, particularly its famous painted ceiling and a Victorian triptych. Also at Bromfield is **Ludlow Racecourse**, where Bronze Age barrows have been brought to light.

Standing in an extensive garden with lovely views to the surrounding hills, **Bromfield Manor** is a former rectory built in 1846 in the Gothic style. For the past seven years it has been the home of John and Christine Mason, who offer outstanding accommodation in two beautifully appointed bedrooms, each with a private bathroom. The twin-bedded room is on the ground floor, the double on the first floor, and both enjoy south-facing views of the Whitcliffe beauty spot. Decor and furnishings throughout are of the highest standard, and guests can relax in a very comfortable lounge. A fine English breakfast starts the day, featuring home-baked bread, home-made preserves and top-quality bacon and sausages from a local butcher. The village and its environs offer plenty to interest historians and lovers of the countryside, and next to the manor stands the 12th century Church of St Mary the Virgin with its famous painted ceiling. This

Bromfield Manor, Bromfield, Ludlow, Shropshire SY8 2JU
Tel & Fax: 01584 856536

really lovely manor, where visitors arrive as guests and leave as friends, is located near the junction of the A49 and A4113 about two miles north of Ludlow. No smoking. No dogs. No children under 12.

A mile or so north of Bromfield, near the River Corve, is the village of **Stanton Lacy** and the Church of St Peter with some Saxon features and Victorian stained glass.

ONIBURY
MAP 2 REF D7

5 miles NW of Ludlow off the A49

A fascinating day out for all the family is guaranteed at **The Wernlas Collection**, a living museum of rare poultry. The setting of this 20-acre smallholding is a joy in itself, and the collection is an internationally acclaimed conservation centre where over 10,000 chicks are hatched each year. Besides the chickens there are rare breeds of goats, sheep and pigs, and some donkeys. The gift shop is themed on chickens - a chickaholic's paradise, in fact. Tel: 01584 856318.

STOKESAY
MAP 2 REF D7

7 miles NW of Ludlow off the A49

The de Say family of nearby Clun started **Stokesay Castle** in about 1240, and a Ludlow wool merchant, Lawrence de Ludlow, made considerable additions, including the Great Hall and fortified south tower. It is the oldest fortified manor house in England and is substantially complete, making it easy to see how a rich medieval merchant would have lived. Entrance to this magnificent building is through a splendid timber-framed gatehouse and the cottage-style gardens are an extra delight. An audio tour guides visitors round the site. Tel: 01588 672544.

The adjacent parish church of St John the Baptist is unusual in having been restored during Cromwell's rule after sustaining severe damage in the Civil War. A remarkable feature in the nave is a series of biblical texts written in giant script on the walls.

CRAVEN ARMS
MAP 2 REF D7

8 miles NW of Ludlow on the A49

The village takes its name from the hotel and pub built by the Earl of Craven. The coming of the railways caused the community to be developed, and it was also at the centre of several roads that were once used by sheep-drovers moving their flocks from Wales to the English markets. In its heyday Craven Arms held one of the largest sheep auctions in Britain, with as many as 20,000 sheep being sold in a single day.

Tucked away off the main road opposite the livestock market, **The Stables Inn** is a real gem, full of old-fashioned charm and a great place to drop in for a drink, a chat and something to eat. The building performed many functions

The Stables Inn, Dale Street West, Craven Arms, Shropshire SY7 9PB
Tel: 01584 672583

down the years, and was for a long time used to stable delivery horses working for the local grocer and the London Tea Company. In the early 1950s it was turned into shop units and saw service as a library, cycle shop, fish & chip shop and antiques dealer. Mike Sykes bought the premises in 1988 and developed the super place it is today. In the bar, amid the beams and plaster and prints, food cooked by Mike is served lunchtime and evening every day, with quality ales (always including a guest ale) to quench the thirst that a walk round the town will generate.

AROUND CRAVEN ARMS

HOPESAY

MAP 2 REF C7

3 miles W of Craven Arms off the B4368

A tiny village, but it's on most maps, which **Hesterworth**, the location of Hesterworth Holidays, is not!

It would be hard to imagine a more picturesque or tranquil setting for a self-catering holiday than the Shropshire Hills, where Sheila and Roger Davies open their house to guests at **Hesterworth Holidays**. Three flats are in the gabled main house, accommodating from 4 to 8 guests, while next to the house round a small courtyard are eight cottages for between 2 and 6 guests, making it an ideal place for groups. The cottages and flats are named after local hills, and

**Hesterworth Holidays, Hesterworth, Near Craven Arms
Shropshire SY7 8EX Tel: 01588 660487 web: www.go2.co.uk/hesterworth**

each has its own character; all are fully equipped for a self-catering holiday, but B&B is also available. Evening meals can be served in the accommodation or in the large dining room. The 12 acres of gardens and grounds, with streams and a pond, are an added delight, especially when the spring flowers start to blossom. Say the owners: "We truly believe that there is no better centre in Britain for the historian, motorist, walker, birdwatcher or simply for people who love the countryside."

CLUN   MAP 2 REF B7
6 miles W of Craven Arms on the A488/B4368

A quiet, picturesque little town in the valley of the River Clun, overlooked by the ruins of its **castle**, which was once the stronghold of the Fitzalan family. The shell of the keep and the earthworks are the main surviving features. The **Church of St George** has a fortress-like tower with small windows and a lovely 17th-century tiered pyramidal top. There are also some splendid Norman arcades with circular pillars and scalloped capitals. The 14th-century north aisle roof and restored nave roof are an impressive sight that will keep necks craning for some time. Some wonderful Jacobean woodwork and a marvellous medieval studded canopy are other sights worth lingering over at this beautiful church, which is a great tribute to GE Street, who was responsible for its restoration in 1876. Geological finds are the main attractions in the little **Local History Museum** in the Town Hall. The real things are to be found on site at **Bury Ditches**,

Clun Church

north of Clun on the way to **Bishop's Castle**. The Ditches are an Iron Age fort on a 7-acre tree-covered site.

Visitors looking for generous helpings of hospitality and first-class food should blaze a trail to **The Buffalo Inn**, which stands in the heart of picturesque Clun at the crossroads of the A488 and B4368. Formerly called the Buffalo Head Hotel, Lorne and Brenda's grand old inn, whose bar and lounge attractively combine period and modern features, is open every session and all day Friday to Sunday in summer, and a snack or full meal can be rustled up both lunchtime and evening. You can eat anywhere, but it's best to book ahead for a table in the dining area, especially at weekends. Everything is home-made, even the chips and the sausages, and chargrilled steaks and chicken are the house specialities. Local brews feature among the ales. For guests staying overnight - Sir Walter Scott

The Buffalo Inn, The Square, Clun, Shropshire SY7 8JA
Tel: 01588 640225

stayed several months while working on one of his novels - there are three lovely bedrooms, all doubles, two with en suite facilities. At the back of the inn is a large garden with views over the valley.

Reg and Judy are the affable owners of **Crown House**, a listed Georgian building that has in previous incarnations been an inn and a saddle and harness-makers workshop. The self-contained B&B accommodation is in the old

Crown House, Church Street, Clun, Shropshire SY7 8JW
Tel: 01588 640780

workshop, which has its own front door; access is through the double gates of the old coach entrance into a secluded flower-filled courtyard. The twin-bedded room has a very generous en suite bathroom, while the double-bedded room, with its original stonework and timbered features, has a shower room and separate toilet. In addition to the two bedrooms there is a large, comfortable residents' lounge/dining room. A traditional English breakfast starts the day, and packed lunches are available on request. A little garden affords delightful views over Clun to the castle and the hills beyond.

High up overlooking Clun, the magnificent **Cockford Hall** enjoys an equally magnificent setting in spectacular woodland that's rich in wildlife and within easy reach of Offa's Dyke Walk. Quality is the keynote here, in both the lovingly

The Dick Turpin Cottage, Cockford Hall, Clun, Shropshire SY7 8LR
Tel: 01588 640327 Fax: 01588 640881

restored Georgian farmhouse nestling in 20 acres on a hillside and in the self-contained cottage known as **The Dick Turpin**. The charm of the Hall, with its many features of historical and architectural interest, has been carefully preserved, but all the modern comforts are also provided, including central heating, double glazing and state-of-the-art radio, CD and TV equipment in the superbly appointed bedrooms. Owner Roger Wren has recently refurbished the spacious cottage (ETB rating de luxe 5 keys), which has a bedroom with a double or two single beds, an en suite bathroom with separate shower and bath, a large sitting room with log fire, and a fully fitted kitchen and laundry. Arrangements can be made for guests to lunch or dine at the Cookhouse Restaurant at Bromfield near Ludlow, which was created by Mr Wren.

Down the valley are other Cluns: **Clunton**, **Clunbury** and **Clungunford**. This quartet was idyllically described by AE Housman in *A Shropshire Lad:*

> *In valleys of springs and rivers,*
> *By Onny and Teme and Clun,*
> *The country for easy livers,*
> *The quietest under the sun.*

ASTON-UNDER-CLUN MAP 2 REF C7
2 miles W of Craven Arms off the B4368

Not one of Housman's Cluns, but well worth a mention and a visit. The village's **Arbor Tree Dressing** ceremony has been held every year since 1786. Following the Battle of Worcester in 1651, King Charles spent some time up a tree (see under Boscobel) and to commemorate his escape he proclaimed Arbor Day, a day in May, as a national holiday when tree-dressing took place. The custom generally died out but was revived here in 1786 when a local landowner married. As Aston was part of his estate he revived the tradition of dressing the Black Poplar in the middle of the village, a custom which still survives.

PURSLOW

MAP 2 REF C7

4 miles W of Craven Arms on the B4368

Standing on the B4368 in the historic village of Purslow, the **Hundred House Inn**, with parts dating back to 1637, was used as a local court until 1914. Good judges today are unanimous in praise of the hospitality and good cheer pro-

**The Hundred House Inn, Purslow, Near Craven Arms, Shropshire SY7 0HJ
Tel: 01588 660541**

vided by Sue and Steve, with Steve's varied menu singled out for particular plaudits. The home-made soups are always in demand, and among the 'all-time favourites' are scampi, chicken tikka masala, lasagne and Thai green chicken curry. Other options include grills, beef in Guinness, omelettes and salads, and there are also plenty of light bites and vegetarian dishes. The bars have enormous old-world appeal, with black beams, a brick fireplace and highly polished rustic chairs and tables. There's good off-road parking and a large beer garden.

BISHOP'S CASTLE

MAP 2 REF C7

9 miles NW of Craven Arms off the A488

This small and ancient town lies in an area of great natural beauty in solitary border country. Little remains of the castle, built in the 12th century for the Bishops of Hereford, which gave the place its name, but there is no shortage of fine old buildings for the visitor to see. The **House on Crutches Museum**, sited in one of the oldest and most picturesque of these buildings, recounts the town's history. Its gable end is supported on wooden posts - hence the name. North of Bishop's Castle lie the **Stiperstones**, a rock-strewn quartzite outcrop rising to a height of 1,700' at the Devil's Chair. A bleak place of brooding solitude, the ridge is part of a 1,000-acre National Nature Reserve and on the lower slopes gaunt chimneys, derelict buildings and neglected roads and paths are silent reminders of the lead-mining industry that flourished here from Roman times until the 19th century. To the west, on the other side of the A49 near **Chirbury**, is **Mitchell's Fold** stone circle, a Bronze Age circle of 15 stones. This is Shropshire's oldest monument, its origins and purpose unknown.

ACTON SCOTT
5 miles N of Craven Arms off the A49

Map 2 ref D7

Signposted off the A49 just south of Church Stretton, **Acton Scott Historic Working Farm** offers a fascinating insight into farming and rural life as practised in the South Shropshire hills at the close of the 19th century. Owned by Shropshire County Council, it is a living museum with a commitment to preserving both traditional farming techniques and rural craft skills. Every day visitors can see milking by hand and butter-making in the dairy. There are weekly visits from the wheelwright, farrier and blacksmith, while in the fields the farming year unfolds with ploughing, sowing and harvesting; special attractions include lambing, shearing, cider-making and threshing with steam and flail.

**Acton Scott Historic Working Farm, Wenlock Lodge, Acton Scott,
Near Church Stretton, Shropshire SY6 6QN
Tel: 01694 781306 Fax: 01694 781569**

The waggoner and his team of heavy horses provide the power to work the land, while the stockman looks after the farm's livestock, among which are many rare breeds of cattle, sheep and pigs.

The year is filled with a splendid programme of crafts and special events, including demonstrations and talks with some hands-on opportunities. Each year brings additional attractions, and 1999 saw the introduction of an enclosed brick kiln where conservation bricks are produced. The School House Café is located in what was the village school, built in the 1860s. It serves a range of light meals, luncheons and afternoon teas, which can also be enjoyed in the cottage garden. The farm shop sells country craft work, souvenirs and ice cream. The farm is open Tuesday to Sunday plus Bank Holiday Mondays, between the beginning of April and the end of October. Most activities are wheelchair-accessible. No dogs. Shropshire County Council also run Ludlow Museum and Much Wenlock Museum (see details under town entries).

CHURCH STRETTON   MAP 2 REF D6
8 miles N of Craven Arms on the A49

The town has a long history - King John granted a charter in 1214 - and traces of the medieval town are to be seen among the 18th and 19th-century buildings in the High Street.

The Kings Arms is John and Netty Barr's first venture into the licensed trade, but in their first year they've already made plenty of new friends and regulars.

The Kings Arms, 53 High Street, Church Stretton, Shropshire SY6 6BY
Tel: 01694 722807

The premises, which are 200 years old, are located in a prominent position on the High Street, and behind the smart whitewashed and timbered facade the pub is roomy enough to be comfortable but small enough to create a lovely cosy atmosphere, with hospitality at a real high. Netty has a fine reputation for the quality of her cooking, and every lunchtime and evening she keeps the customers happy with a good choice of dishes from the menu and the specials list. The pub also keeps a good range of ales, which always include a guest ale. Children welcome.

Elsewhere in the town, many of the black-and-white timbered buildings are not so old as they look, having been built at the turn of the century when the town had ideas of becoming a health resort. Just behind the High Street stands the **Church of St Laurence**, with Saxon foundations, a Norman nave and a tower dating from about 1200. Over the aisle is a memorial to a tragic event that happened in 1968 when three boys were killed in a fire. The memorial is in the form of a gridiron, with flakes of copper simulating flames. The gridiron is the symbol of St Laurence, who was burnt to death on one in AD258. The Victorian novelist Sarah Smith, who wrote under the name of Hesba Stretton, was a frequent visitor to nearby All Stretton, and there is a small memorial window to her in the south transept.

Tucked away above a ladies' outfitters just off the main street is a real hidden gem. **Acorn Wholefood Restaurant & Coffee House**, created ten years ago by

Acorn Wholefood Restaurant & Coffee House, 26 Sandford Avenue, Church Stretton, Shropshire SY6 6BW. Tel: 01694 722495

Chris Bland and run by Chris and her mother Gwen, specialises in all kinds of wholefood dishes in which quality is the over-riding consideration. Mass production has no meaning here, and Chris never caters for 'popular tastes'; she continually experiments with her recipes, making everything except the bread, and every item is a labour of love on a menu that runs from marvellous scones and cakes to scone-based pizza, nut roast and a dish of the day for both vegetarians and meat/fish-eaters. Beverages include an impressive list of speciality teas. There are seats inside for 44, and another 30 can sit in the pretty garden. Open 9.30-5.30 (till 6 in summer). Closed Tuesday, also Wednesday except during school holidays. No smoking.

A mile from the town centre are **Carding Mill Valley** and the **Long Mynd**. The valley and the moorland into which it runs are National Trust property and very popular for walking and picnicking. This wild area of heath affords marvellous views across Shropshire to the Cheshire Plains and the Black Mountains. Tea room, shop, information centre. Tel: 01694 723068.

LITTLE STRETTON   MAP 2 REF D6
2 miles S of Church Stretton on the B4370

The village of Little Stretton nestles in the **Stretton Gap**, with the wooded slopes of Ragleth to the east and **Long Mynd** to the west. It is a peaceful spot, bypassed by the A49, and is a delightful place to stroll for a stroll. The most photographed building is **All Saints Church**, with a black and white timbered frame, a thatched roof and the general look of a cottage rather than a church. When built in 1903 it had an iron roof, but this was soon found to be too noisy and was soon replaced with thatch (heather initially, then the straw that tops it today). Among many other interesting buildings are **Manor House**, a cruck hall dating from 1500, and **Bircher Cottage**, of a similar vintage.

"Switzerland without the wolves and avalanches" is a description sometimes applied to this beautiful, serene part of the world, and there is no finer base for enjoying it than Paul and Louise Oatham's **Mynd House**. Built in 1902, it became a small hotel of quality in 1987 and continues to meet the demands of discerning visitors. The seven bedrooms are right out of the top drawer; all with bathrooms en suite, they include two superb suites, one with a conservatory, four-poster bed and double corner spa bath. Most look out on to fantastic views across Stretton Gap to Ragleth Hill, an extinct volcano. There are two comfortable lounges, and a bar lounge in which to enjoy a drink whilst studying the evening's menu. The food here is as outstanding as the accommodation, offering the best of home-grown recipes and some delights from Europe and further afield. The hotel is rightly proud of its cellar, which has won many awards; the wine list runs to more than 300 bins, including over 100 halves, and a good selection of dessert wines and ports by the glass. The restaurant is open to non-residents, but reservations are essential. This is great walking country, and a

Mynd House, Little Stretton, Near Church Stretton, Shropshire SY6 6RB
Tel: 01694 722212 Fax: 01694 724180 web: go2.co.uk/myndhouse
e-mail: myndhouse@go2.co.uk

booklet is available detailing six walks starting from the hotel. It is also an ideal touring base, with Ironbridge, Ludlow and Shrewsbury among the abundance of easily-reached attractions. Closed January.

WENTNOR   Map 2 ref C6
3 miles W of Church Stretton on minor roads

Wentnor lies beyond the western edge of the Long Mynd, on the River East Onny.

A real gem of a village pub, its outside festooned with flowers and plants, **The Crown Inn** is run in fine style by Simon and Joanna Beadman. It dates back all the way to the 16th century, and among the beams and brasses, the bar is a cheerful spot to meet for a drink and a chat. In the 35-cover restaurant - best to book on Friday and Saturday evenings - waitress service brings Joanna's excellent cooking to the tables. A blackboard lists the day's choices, which typically could include Stilton-topped baked mushrooms, home-made paté, spaghetti carbonara, cod with a cheese sauce and Shrewsbury lamb. Vegetarians will be

The Crown Inn, Wentnor, Shropshire SY9 5EE
Tel: 01588 650613 Fax: 01588 650436 e-mail: crown@lydbury.co.uk

pleased with a choice of three main courses. A large part of the restaurant is designated non-smoking. The Crown also boasts three outstanding letting bedrooms with en suite bath or separate shower room, making it an ideal base for touring this lovely part of the country and its many places of interest.

A short drive north of Church Stretton, on minor roads off the A49, is **Acton Burnell**, where Parliament met in the reign of King Edward 1. It has a small but interesting castle, which, like Stokesay, was a fortified residence rather than a fortress.

CRAVEN ARMS TO BRIDGNORTH

ASTON MUNSLOW   MAP 2 REF D7
6 miles NE of Craven Arms off the B4368

Motorists driving along the B4368 between Craven Arms and Bridgnorth should definitely make a point of stopping at the **Swan Inn**. Believed to be one of the oldest hostelries in Shropshire, it has a history going back to the middle of the 14th century, and its whitewashed face, with timbers and some odd angles, is

**The Swan Inn, Aston Munslow, Near Craven Arms, Shropshire SY7 9ER
Tel: 01584 841415**

matched inside for period charm by flagstones, beams, brasses and an inglenook fireplace with massive stone surround. It's open all day, every day, with very good food always available. Booking is advised for a table in the restaurant, which has just 16 covers, but food is served throughout. Baguettes and toasties, burgers, pies and jacket potatoes make excellent quick snacks, while the main menu includes steaks, cod in batter, game casserole and chicken curries at various heat levels. Children's dishes are also available. Naughty things like spotted dick or treacle sponge fill any remaining gaps. A traditional roast is the centrepiece of Sunday lunch. Next to the main building is the old coach house, which the inn's owners Will and Sharon Williams plan to turn into another eating area and B&B accommodation. They also own a nearby farm, where cider is produced for sale at the inn.

MORVILLE   MAP 3 REF F6
3 miles W of Bridgnorth on the A458

Morville Hall, 16th-century with 18th-century additions, stands at the junction of the A458 and B4368. Within its grounds, the **Dower House Garden** is a 1 1/2-acre site designed by Dr Katherine Swift and begun in 1989. Its aim is to tell the history of English gardens in a sequence of separate gardens designed in the style of different historical periods. Particular attention is given to the use of authentic plants and construction techniques. Old roses are a speciality of the garden. Tel: 01746 714407. Parking is available in the churchyard of the fine Norman Church of St Gregory, which is also well worth a visit.

New tenants Richard and Charlotte Vowell bring a wealth of experience and plenty of imaginative ideas to their latest enterprise, the 18th-century **Acton**

The Acton Arms, Haughton Lane, Morville, Near Bridgnorth, Shropshire WV16 4RJ Tel: 01746 714209

Arms. Behind a whitewashed frontage with cheerful window boxes are the village bar, a separate lounge and a light, roomy restaurant. A couple of picnic bench tables are set out at the front, and behind the pub is a beer garden. Prime fresh produce is used for home-cooked lunches and dinners on menus that change every day and always provide a really ample choice. The pub is located on the A458 three miles north of Bridgnorth, in a village best known for the National Trust Dower House Garden (see above).

Another fine Norman church is located in nearby **Aston Eyre**. A tympanum over the doorway represents Christ's entry into Jerusalem and shows him sitting not astride his mount but sideways. He is flanked by two men, one with a young ass, the other spreading palm leaves.

BRIDGNORTH

The ancient market town of Bridgnorth, straddling the River Severn, comprises **Low Town**, and, 100 feet up sandstone cliffs, **High Town**. 1101 is a key date in its history, when the **Norman Castle** was built by Robert de Belesme from Quatt. All that remains of the castle is part of the keep tower, which leans at an angle of about 15 degrees as a result of an attempt to demolish it after the Civil War. The castle grounds offer splendid views of the river, and when King Charles 1 stayed here in 1642 he declared the view from the **Castle Walk** to be the finest in his dominion. The **Bridgnorth Museum** (Tel: 01746 763358) is a good place to start a tour of this interesting town. It occupies rooms over the arches of the **North Gate**, which is the only one of the town's original fortifications to survive - though most of it was rebuilt in the 18th century. The **Costume and Childhood Museum** (Tel: 01746 764636) incorporates a costume gallery, a complete Victorian nursery and a collection of rare minerals. It's a really charming place that appeals to all ages. The Civil War caused great damage in Bridgnorth and the lovely **Town Hall** is one of many timber-framed buildings put up just after the war. The sandstone arched base was completed in 1652 and later covered in brick; Charles ll took a great interest in it and when improvements were needed he made funds available from his own purse and from a collection he ordered be made in every parish in England.

Tucked away off the High Street, behind the old Town Hall, there's a real

little gem in the shape of **The Bakehouse Café**, where Pam, Paul and Tim Larvin provide daytime refreshment in delightfully friendly, relaxed surroundings. The two little rooms (36 covers on two floors) are cool in summer and very comfortable, an ideal place to take a break from shopping or sightseeing. The menu offers scones, cakes and made-to-order sandwiches to accompany a good cup of tea or coffee, with cooked breakfasts and jacket potatoes for something more substantial; and there's always a selection of daily specials to increase the choice. Open 9-5 Monday to Saturday, 11.30-5 Sunday.

The Bakehouse Café, Central Court, off High Street, Bridgnorth, Shropshire WV16 4DX Tel: 01746 761221

The Bell & Talbot is a 250-year-old coaching inn just a short walk from High Street shopping and the Severn Valley Railway. Behind the solid brick facade many original features have been retained, with oak beams throughout, and bar counters hand carved from solid oak. Open log fires warm the bars, where wholesome hot snacks are accompanied by cask ales, including Marstons and Morrells, approved by CAMRA

**The Bell & Talbot, Salop Street, Bridgnorth, Shropshire WV16 4QU
Tel: 01746 763233**

and kept in top condition. Owners Joan and Geoff Bodenham have run the pub for six years, and Geoff's background as a professional musician and singer inspired the major attraction of live music on Thursday, Saturday and Sunday, with jazz, folk, blues and rock 'n' roll all featured. For guests staying overnight there are three comfortable bedrooms, each with adjoining toilet and shower unit. During the summer months the colourful patio around the original public house well is a popular spot.

St Mary's Street is one of the three streets off High Street which formed the planned new town of the 12th century. Many of the houses, brick faced over timber frames, have side passages leading to gardens which contained workshops and cottages. **Bishop Percy's House** is the oldest house standing in the town, a handsome building dating from 1580 and one of the very few timber-framed houses to survive the fire of 1646. It is named after the Reverend Dr Percy, who was born in the house in 1729 and became Bishop of Dromore.

For many visitors the most irresistible attraction in Bridgnorth is the **Castle Hill Cliff Railway**, funicular railway built in 1892 to link the two parts of the town. The track is 200' long and rises over 100' up the cliff. Originally it operated on a water balance system but it was converted in 1943 to electrically driven colliery-type winding gear. John Betjeman likened a ride on this lovely little railway to a journey up to heaven. For all but the very energetic it might feel like heaven compared to the alternative ways of getting from Low to High Town - seven sets of steps or Cartway, a meandering street that's steeped in history.

No visit to historic Bridgnorth would be complete without dropping in at **Quaints Vegetarian Bistro**, where Linda Caddick offers a tempting variety of home-cooked dishes catering mainly, though not exclusively, for vegetarians.

Inside the Grade ll listed building the surroundings are cosy and traditional, the walls hung with an exhibition of works by local artists. Morning coffee is accompanied by a wide range of mouthwatering scones and cakes, and savoury snacks include soup, sandwiches and omelettes. In the evening the bistro spreads its wings with full menus for both vegetarian and non-vegetarian diners. The premises are licensed for beer and wine, both of which are available in organic or traditional varieties. Opening hours are 10.30-3.30 and 6.30-9.30.

The bridge across the Severn, rebuilt in 1823 to a Thomas Telford design, has a clock tower with an inscription commemorating the building, in 1808, of the first steam locomotive at John Hazeldine's foundry a short distance upstream.

Quaints Vegetarian Bistro, 69 St Mary's Street, Bridgnorth, Shropshire WV16 4DR. Tel: 01746 768980

Talking of steam locomotives, Bridgnorth is the northern terminus of the wonderful **Severn Valley Railway** (see under Bewdley for more details).

The Old Mill Antique Centre, which opened in 1996, stands between one of the main roads into town and the banks of the River Severn. The centre is run by brothers Denis and John Ridgway, who also own a sister company of Auctioneers and Valuers. The substantial Grade ll listed building, used previously as

**The Old Mill Antique Centre, 48 Mill Street, Bridgnorth,
Shropshire WV15 5AG Tel: 01746 768778 Fax: 01746 768944**

a seed mill, is fronted by a 16th century town house, and extensive refurbishment has made it an attractive site for dealers in all areas of antiques and retailers of quality reproduction furniture. More than 40,000 square feet of space, laid out over three floors, display a huge variety of furniture, fittings, silver, porcelain, clocks, jewellery and many other collectables spanning the last 200 years. Items start at around £5 and reach well into five figures, so pockets of every depth are catered for. The centre, which is open seven days a week, has a tearoom selling sandwiches, home-made cakes, vegetarian dishes and daily specials.

Owner Simon Daymond-Harris and his staff set high standards at the 17th century **Down Inn**, which as a founder member of the Campaign for Real Food uses nothing but the best natural ingredients, locally sourced wherever possible. Behind the sturdy greystone facade the scene is a traditional one, with wood panelling, upholstered highback chairs, an assortment of tables of all shapes and sizes, and a collection of old port bottles. The blackboard menu makes mouthwatering reading, and with everything guaranteed made to order the final choice can pose a very pleasant problem! Speciality dishes appear each week, and there are always main courses for vegetarians; individual dietary re-

The Down Inn, Ludlow Road, Bridgnorth, Shropshire WV16 6UA
Tel: 01746 789624 Fax: 01746 789539
e-mail: downinn@downinn.screaming.net

quirements can be met with advance notice. Booking is advisable at peak times at the weekend, when food is served all day. The inn, which enjoys lovely views from its large beer garden, stands on the B4364 Ludlow road three miles south-west of Bridgnorth.

AROUND BRIDGNORTH - SOUTH

EARDINGTON
1 mile S of Bridgenorth on the B4555

MAP 3 REF F6

Eardington is a southern suburb of Bridgnorth, where, a mile out of town on the B4555, stands **Daniel's Mill**, a picturesque working watermill powered by an enormous (38') wheel. Family-owned for 200 years, the mill still produces flour. Tel: 01746 762753

Over the last few years Sue Lucas and her business partner Mark have built up an enviable reputation for excellent food and accommodation at **The Swan Inn**. Just five minutes south of Bridgnorth on the B4555, the setting provides lovely views along the River Severn, which flows only 400 yards away, and there are plenty of sights to be seen in the vicinity. The Swan, built in the 17th century and extended in the 1970s, is one of the Severn Valley Railway's offi-cially recommended hostelries, and the two cosy bars, kept warm in winter by log fires, are great places to swap railway reminiscences over a glass of real ale. In the restaurant, where booking is advisable at weekends, Mark produces a fine

The Swan Inn, Knowle Sands, Eardington, Bridgnorth,
Shropshire WV16 5JL Tel: 01746 763424 e-mail: sueswan@hotmail.com

choice of grills, fish dishes, vegetarian options and luscious desserts on a menu
that's supplemented by daily specials such as beef medallions with a blue cheese
glaze. There's also a wide range of bar snacks, and the superb food - the restaurant was recently nominated the best in the area - is accompanied by a full
selection of wines. Food theme nights are held regularly, and each month there's
an evening of live music. When the weather permits, food is served out on the
lovely patio. The five well-equipped bedrooms, four of them with en suite facilities, include family rooms with an extra bed. Disabled access to the bars and
bedrooms. Ample parking.

The Halfway House Inn is a 17th-century hostelry standing on the B4363
just over a mile from the centre of Bridgnorth. The story goes that Queen Victoria, as a young princess, was travelling past here on her way from Worcester to
Shrewsbury when she asked where she was. "Halfway there" came the reply,
and thus the inn got its name. The bar is small and cosy, with nice old furniture,
an inglenook fireplace and a tiny serving hatch. At the back is a roomy restaurant where good-value lunchtime and evening meals (booking advisable) are
accompanied by local ales and a decent selection of wines. Peter Williams and
his family have increased the appeal of this delightful place by making available
three adjoining holiday cottages to add to the two three-bedded en suite letting
rooms upstairs at the inn. Also next to the inn is a 10-berth caravan park, where

The Halfway House Inn, Cleobury Road, Eardington,
Near Bridgnorth, Shropshire WV16 5LS Tel: 01746 762670
Web: www.pengwernsportstours.com

a shower block and a disabled toilet have recently been built. Summer weekends bring scores of visitors for sporting activity holidays which the owners arrange.

QUATT
MAP 3 REF G7

4 miles SE of Bridgnorth on the A442

Quatt is the location of the National Trust's **Dudmaston Hall**, a late 17th-century house with fine furniture, Dutch flower paintings, modern pictures and sculptures (Hepworth, Moore), botanical art, watercolours, family and natural history and colourful gardens with lakeside walks, a rockery and a wooded valley. Tel: 01746 780866. The church at Quatt contains some splendid monuments and memorials to the Wolryche family.

Nearby, in the grounds of Stanmore Hall on the Stourbridge road, is the **Midland Motor Museum**, with an outstanding collection of more than 100 vehicles, mostly sports and racing cars. Tel: 01746 762992. The grounds also include a touring caravan site.

WOOTTON
MAP 3 REF G7

3 miles SE of Bridgnorth between the A458 and A442

In a pretty village just south of Bridgnorth stands **The Cider House**, where Brian and Kath Jervis have based themselves since 1986. The premises were first

The Cider House, Wootton, Near Bridgnorth, Shropshire WV15 6EB
Tel: 01746 780285 Fax: 01746 780199

licensed to sell cider in 1846, and that's what they do to this day - this is the original pub with no beer! In the bar, adorned with local scenes and a collection of clay pipes, or out in the cider garden, a good choice of high-quality ciders can be enjoyed, including an increasingly popular non-alcoholic variety. Cider can also be bought to take away. Filled rolls and savoury pies are the main items on the menu, which expands at weekends to include barbecues. The owners have operated mobile cider bars from these premises for many years, taking them to outdoor functions covering the length and breadth of the land. The Midland Motor Museum, just five minutes away, is one of many local attractions.

SIX ASHES
MAP 3 REF G7

4 miles SE of Bridgnorth on the A458

Six Ashes Tea Rooms & Restaurant is a great place for a break on the A458 road between Bridgnorth and Stourbridge. Sandra and Barrie Bromley are the friendly proprietors, in residence here since the autumn of 1998 after a lifetime in the business of restoring vintage cars. The 19th century cottages have seen service as a shop, a filling station and a post office, and in their current role comprise a 20-seat restaurant and an 18-seat tea room, both with beams and pretty cottage-style furnishings. Motorists, walkers and cyclists take the opportunity to drop in for a snack, and members of the WI are among the regulars who enjoy the peaceful, civilised atmosphere and the wholesome fare on offer. A big breakfast is served until 1 o'clock, and sandwiches, salads, soup, ploughman's and jacket potatoes are supplemented by daily hot specials marked up on the blackboard.

**Six Ashes Tea Rooms & Restaurant, Broad Oak, Six Ashes,
Near Bridgnorth, Shropshire WV15 6EQ Tel: 01384 221216**

On the sweeter side are home-made cakes and gateaux, teacakes, scones and a cream tea. To drink, there are speciality teas, cafetière coffee, milkshakes and beer or wine by the glass. Booking is advisable, particularly for the Sunday roast served between 12 and 2.30. Opening times are 10-5 Tuesday-Sunday, and 7-10 Friday & Saturday evenings. The tea room is recommended by the AA and the Teapot Trail, and has the Seal of Approval of the National Tea Council.

BURWARTON   Map 3 ref E7
5 miles SW of Bridgnorth on the B4364

Burwarton stands in lovely countryside on the road that links Bridgnorth and Ludlow, near Brown Clee hill.

Easy to find on the B4364 Ludlow-Bridgnorth road, **The Boyne Arms** is a great place to stop for a drink, a meal or an overnight stay. The views are delightful, the scenery superb, and nearby Brown Clee is the highest spot in the whole county, so walkers can work up a good thirst and appetite before a visit to Richard and Janet Grant's beautiful old coaching inn. Food is served every session except Sunday evening, and Janet's repertoire really does include something for everyone, with fresh local produce very much to the fore. Excellent real ales and country wines can be enjoyed with a meal or on their own, and coffee and tea are available all day. Food can be eaten either inside, where a selection of paintings and prints by local artists takes the eye, or out in the lovely terraced garden, which includes a small and very discreet adventure playground. Guests staying in the four spacious bedrooms (one with an unusual sit-in bath) are

**The Boyne Arms, Burwarton, Near Bridgnorth, Shropshire WV16 6QH
Tel: 01746 787214**

brought tea in the morning - a good start to the day in this lovely part of the world. The Burwarton Show, held annually in August, is one of the largest one-day agricultural shows in the country.

BILLINGSLEY   MAP 3 REF F7

5 miles S of Bridgnorth on the B4363

In a beautiful wooded valley near the village, **Rays Farm Country Matters** is home to many farm animals including Highland cattle, deer, donkeys, goats and pigs, plus more than 50 owls. Tel: 01299 841255. The longest bridleway in Shropshire, and one of the longest in the country, starts at the farm. This is the **Jack Mytton Way**, named after a 19th-century hard-living squire and sometime MP for Shrewsbury. It runs all the way to Llanfair Waterdine in the Teme Valley, a distance of some 70 miles.

HIGHLEY   MAP 3 REF F7

6 miles S of Bridgnorth off the A442 or B4555

The village has a stop on the **Severn Valley Railway**.

New owner Kevin Ahern has transformed **The Malt Shovel** from an ordinary pub into something rather special, adding bedrooms and a conservatory and landscaping the gardens. Its appeal has thus been considerably widened, and attracts not only an increasing number of local regulars but also tourists and walkers on some of the oldest-established trails in the region. The three-storey building stands at the north end of the village a mile from the River Severn, and the views from the sun terrace are superb. There's plenty of space both inside and out, and children can spend a happy hour or two in the adventure playground. The food on offer covers a good spread, from bar snacks to a full à la carte menu served in the 50-seat restaurant. Local real ales will quench

The Malt Shovel, Woodhill Road, Highley, Near Bridgnorth, Shropshire WV16 6HT Tel: 01746 862550

the biggest thirst, and there are some decent wines to accompany a meal. Above the pub are six lovely double-bedded letting rooms which share two bathrooms.

STODDESDON
MAP 3 REF F7

7 miles S of Bridgnorth on minor roads off the B4363/4

Country roads lead off the B4363 and B4364 to the peaceful village of Stottesdon and a real gem of a pub called **The Fighting Cocks**. This lovely pub has a history going back to the middle of the 18th century and part of it was once a

The Fighting Cocks, High Street, Stottesdon, Shropshire DY14 8TZ. Tel: 01746 718270

slaughterhouse that contained a cockpit. The wheel that used to hoist the animals to slaughter is now a feature in the raised area at one end of the pub. The whole place has tremendous character and old-world charm, and it's a popular stop with walkers, cyclists and motorists, as well as being a local favourite. In the small, cosy restaurant (book for Friday or Saturday) or anywhere else in the pub, excellent home cooking covers a good range of dishes that always include at least half a dozen daily specials. All the cooking is done by owner Sandra Jefferies, whose sons help to run the pub. Three bitters are always available, with one guest ale from a micro-brewery, plus a good selection of lager, stout and mild.

AROUND BRIDGNORTH - NORTH

MUCH WENLOCK
8 miles NW of Bridgnorth on the A458

MAP 2 REF E6

The narrow streets of Much Wenlock are a delight to explore, and among the mellow buildings are some absolute gems. The **Guildhall** is one of them, dating from 1540 and added to in 1577 with a chamber over the stone medieval prison. The Guildhall was until recently used as a courtroom, and the Town Council still meets here once a month. The **Museum** (Tel: 01952 727773) is housed in the former market hall, which was built in 1878. There are interesting displays on the geology, flora and fauna of **Wenlock Edge** (see below), as well as local history items including Dr William Penny Brookes's Olympian Games. A forerunner of, and inspiration for the Olympic Games, they are an annual event in the town every year, having started in 1850. The good doctor lived in what is now Lloyds Bank.

Holy Trinity Church, 'mother' to ten churches in villages around Much Wenlock, is a dominant presence in the town, though less conspicuous than it was until 1931, when its spire was removed. Its nave and chancel are Norman, the porch 13th-century. The Parish Registers date from 1558.

The sight that simply must not be missed on a visit here is the ruins of the **Priory of St Milburga**. The Priory was originally a nunnery, founded in the 7th century by a Mercian princess and destroyed some 200 years later. Leofric, Earl of Mercia and husband of Lady Godiva, re-established it as a priory in 1050 and the current spectacular ruins belong to the Cluniac Priory rebuilt in the 12th and 13th centuries. The best remaining features are the wall carvings in the cloisters and the Norman interlacing of arches and doorways in the Chapter House. **The Prior's Lodge**, dating from about 1500, is particularly impressive with its steeply pitched roof of sandstone tiles above the rows of mullioned windows. Away from the main site is **St Milburga's Well**, whose waters are reputed to cure eye diseases.

Wenlock Priory

Easy to find in the main street of medieval Much Wenlock, **The Wheatland Fox** is thriving under owner Malcolm Hammond and his son Miles, offering a warm welcome, good food and drink, and a comfortable overnight stay. The building, Grade ll listed, dates from 1669, with a Georgian frontage added soon afterwards. It is now smartly painted in white, with an eye-catching sign of the dashing Mr Fox in hunting garb. Old oak beams are a feature in the seven bed-rooms, each with its own style and character (some antiques), and all with private bathroom en suite, colour TV, radio-alarm, tea/coffee-maker, direct-dial tel-ephone, minibar and central heating. Two of the rooms are suitable for family occupation. There are beams, too, in the delightful dining room, where an open fire adds to the relaxed, welcoming atmosphere. The walls are adorned with the work of local artists - paintings and prints that are all for sale. Top-quality local produce plays an important part on the monthly-changing menu, which offers a winning combination of dishes both familiar and more unusual, all prepared to order: potato and flat-leaf parsley soup laced with truffle oil; mascarpone

**The Wheatland Fox Hotel, High Street, Much Wenlock,
Shropshire TF13 6AD Tel: 01952 727292 Fax: 01952 727301**

cheese and kipper pancake; herb-crusted rack of lamb; cod fillet with cheesy mashed potato, spinach and a chilli and onion salsa; goat's cheese and courgette parcels. Bar snacks are served at lunchtime, and a good choice of wines and real ales complements the fine food.

WENLOCK EDGE   MAP 2 REF E6
4 miles S of Much Wenlock on the B4371

Wenlock Edge is one of the most spectacular and impressive landmarks in the whole county, a limestone escarpment dating back 400 million years and a paradise for naturalists and lovers of the outdoors. It runs for 15 miles all the way down to Craven Arms. For centuries its quarries have produced the stone used in many of the local buildings; it was also a source of lime for agricultural fertiliser and much went into the blast furnaces that fired the Industrial Revolution.

The welcome is warm and natural at the Waring family's **Wenlock Edge Inn**, which offers all the assets of a traditional hostelry - good food and drink, genial company and comfortable overnight accommodation. Under the beams and warmed by a fire in the inglenook, visitors can enjoy genuine home cooking of classic British dishes such as bradan rost (hot-smoked salmon) served with organic bread, then a main dish often of local origin, perhaps Shrewsbury lamb or Shropshire venison pie, rounding things off with a scrumptious dessert like Queen of Puddings or a super crumble. The three bedrooms are all en suite,

The Wenlock Edge Inn, Hill Top, Wenlock Edge, Shropshire TF13 6DJ
Tel: 01746 785678 Fax: 01746 785285
Internet: www.go2.co.uk/wenlockedgeinn email: jpwonwei@enta.net

one a separate cottage. The final plus at this truly delightful old inn - formerly quarrymen's cottages - is the peaceful setting with commanding views and National Trust walks.

7 Around Shrewsbury

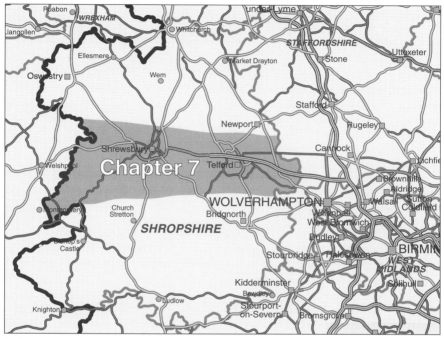

© MAPS IN MINUTES ™ (1998)

This chapter visits the county capital Shrewsbury and the Ironbridge Gorge, which saw the birth of the industrial revolution. It now houses some of the most fascinating and evocative museums in the whole country

BROSELEY   MAP 3 REF F5
4 miles NE of Much Wenlock on the B4373

A short ride or an invigorating walk takes us from Chapter 6 towards the heart of the Industrial Revolution. Broseley, which stands on the south side of the River Severn opposite Ironbridge, was the headquarters of John Wilkinson, the great ironmaster and head of a giant empire. It was while he was living at **The Lawns** in Broseley that he commissioned the Shrewsbury architect Thomas Pritchard to design the world's first iron bridge. He also launched the first iron boat, *The Trial*, on the Severn in 1787 and even designed his own iron coffin.

Broseley was the centre of an ancient local industry in clay products and tobacco pipes, and the **Pipe Museum** (Tel: 01952 882445), untouched for more than 40 years, is a time-capsule factory where the famous Broseley Churchwarden pipes were made until 1957. Just north of Broseley, off the B4375, on a plateau above a gorge, stands **Benthall Hall**, a 16th-century building in the care of the National Trust, with mullioned windows and a magnificent interior with a carved oak staircase, elaborate plaster ceilings and the Benthall family's collection of furniture, ceramics and paint-

Bottle Kiln, Broseley Pipe Museum

ings. There's a carefully restored plantsman's garden and, in the grounds, an interesting Restoration church. Tel: 01952 882159.

IRONBRIDGE AND IRONBRIDGE GORGE   MAP 3 REF F5
4 miles NE of Much Wenlock on the B4373

This is it, the town at the centre of Ironbridge Gorge, an area which has been designated a World Heritage Centre by UNESCO, ranking it alongside the likes of the Pyramids, the Grand Canyon and the Taj Mahal. It was the first British site on the list. The **bridge** itself is a pedestrian right of way with a tollgate at

The Iron Bridge

one end, and the series of museums that spread along the banks of the Severn in **Ironbridge, Coalbrookdale, Coalport** and **Jackfield** pay tribute to the momentous events that took place here 250 years ago. The first iron wheels were made here, and also the first iron rails and the first steam railway locomotive.

The **IronbridgeVisitor Centre** offers the ideal introduction to the attractions, and plenty of time should be devoted to the individual museums. The **Museum of Iron** in Coalbrookdale in the most historic part of the valley shows the whole story of ironmaking. Next to it is the original furnace used by Abraham Darby when he first smelted iron with coke; a little way north are **Rosehill House,** one of the homes of the Darby family, and **Dale House,** where Abraham Darby's grandson made his plans for the iron bridge.

Built in 1784 as a commercial hotel with stabling, the **Tontine Hotel** is situated immediately opposite the historic Iron Bridge, and is itself steeped in history. Preservation orders ensure that this ruggedly handsome building has changed very little in structure and appearance over the years, and the first striking feature inside is in the foyer, where the magnificent tiled floor has been kept intact and pristine since the day it was laid with tiles supplied by Maw & Co. of nearby Jackfield. Something else that hasn't changed is the warm and friendly service offered by the Tontine management and staff. Trish and John do everything possible to make sure that their guests have an enjoyable stay, even helping to plan sightseeing excursions in this area so full of things to see and do. There are

The Tontine Hotel, The Square, Ironbridge, Shropshire TF8 7AL
Tel: 01952 432127 Fax: 01952 432094

12 very comfortable, well-equipped bedrooms spanning singles, twins, doubles and family rooms. Eight are en suite, and most enjoy views of the bridge. In the bar, a relaxing spot for a drink and a snack, hangs a wealth of paintings of local scenes and events, including the River Severn Frozen Over and the Coracle Man. For a more formal meal, the restaurant, also overlooking the bridge, is open to non-residents seven days a week.

The Old Police Station, owned by John and Lynn Youngman, is one of Ironbridge's less well known museums, but one that is well worth a visit, and for a variety of reasons. The Victorian station and its cells have been painstakingly restored to provide a fascinating insight into the judicial and prison systems at the turn of the century. After it closed for duty in 1964 it was used for various purposes before becoming home to police memorabilia from handcuffs and truncheons to uniforms and documents. The cells are particularly arresting - Cell 4 was the birching centre for Shropshire, and a birching stool still stands in the middle of the room. In the upper-floor theatre, using the unique backdrop of the former station and courthouse, Courthouse Productions put on a wide variety of corporate and personal events, from plays with a buffet supper to Courtroom trial re-enactments; from Victorian Music Halls to Jazz and other musical events. Also on the premises is a tearoom where home baking, traditional afternoon teas and a Victorian buffet are among the offerings. Weddings

**The Old Police Station, 57 Waterloo Street, Ironbridge,
Shropshire TF8 7AA Tel: 01952 433838**

are catered for at the station, and for an eve-of-wedding night with a difference the groom and best man can spend a night in the cells after the evening's celebrations, then wake up to a healthy breakfast before being delivered in style to the church! Also to be found in the Police Station is the **Left Centre**, which holds a vast stock of knives, scissors, kitchen tools and writing aids for left-handers, plus anti-clockwise clocks and 'the best of ambidextrous'.

The Grove Inn was the first commercial hotel in the Ironbridge Gorge, and its scope has now expanded to include the Fat Frog Restaurant (booking recommended: Tel 01952 432240). The proprietors are Gaye Pope and Frenchman Johnny Coleau, who have created a little corner of France in the restaurant with its hand-painted murals, pottery frogs and red check tablecloths. Johnny's menu is a regularly changing selection of English, Continental and vegetarian dishes, with traditional roasts the centrepiece of Sunday lunch. The murals are also a feature in the bars, where food from the restaurant's kitchen is available every day. Overnight guests can choose between four en suite bedrooms and two self-catering flats. Outside, there's waiter service in the Continental-style patio garden.

The Grove Inn, 10 Wellington Road, Coalbrookdale, Near Ironbridge, Shropshire TF8 7DX Tel: 01952 433269

The inn is located next to the Coalbrookdale Museum, which is part of the nearby Ironbridge Gorge Museum.

Ironbridge Open Air Museum of Steel Sculpture

Also at Coalbrookdale is the **Ironbridge Open Air Museum of Steel Sculpture**, a collection of 60 modern steel sculptures of all shapes and sizes set in 10 acres of beautiful countryside.

The **Jackfield Tile Museum,** on the south bank, stands on the site of a world centre of the tile-making industry. The museum houses a fine collection of wall and floor tiles from Victorian times to the 1950s. Demonstrations of traditional tile-making take place regularly. Back across a footbridge to the **Coalport China Museum**, with its marvellous displays of two centuries of porcelain. Coalport was once one of the country's largest manufacturers of porcelain, starting life here but moving its factory to Stoke in the 1920s. Nearby is the extraordinary **Tar Tunnel** with its gushing spring of natural bitumen. It was a popular attraction for tourists in the 18th century, and it remains one of the most interesting geological phenomena in Britain. The tunnel was started in 1786, under the direction of ironmaster William Reynolds, who intended that it should be used for a canal to reach the shafts to the coal seams ¾ of a mile away on Blists Hill. After they had driven the tunnel about 300 yards the miners struck a spring of natural bitumen. Reynolds immediately recognised the scientific interest of the discovery and sent samples of the bitumen to eminent scientists, who declared that the properties of the bitumen were superior to those of tar made of coal. The tunnel was almost forgotten over the years, but in 1965 the Shropshire Mining Club persuaded the owner of the village shop in

Blists Hill

Coalport to let them explore the darkness which lay beyond a door opening from his cellar. They rediscovered the Tar Tunnel, but it was another 18 years before visitors were allowed access to a brief stretch.

At **Blists Hill Victorian Town** visitors can experience the atmosphere and way of life of a working Victorian community; there's a shop, domestic animals, a squatter's cottage, a schoolhouse and a bank which distributes its own legal tender.

Passport tickets are available to admit holders to all the Ironbridge Gorge Museums. Tel: 01952 433522.

Two miles west of Ironbridge, on a minor road off the B4378, stands **Buildwas Abbey**, one of the finest ruined abbeys in England. After 850 years the church is virtually complete except for the roof, and the setting, in a meadow by the Severn against a backdrop of wooded grounds, is both peaceful and evocative. The place is full of things of interest, like the lead-glazed tiles depicting animals and birds in the Chapter House.

Buildwas Abbey

TELFORD

Telford is a sprawling modern development that took several existing towns in the region of the Shropshire coalfield. **Wellington, Hadley, Ketley, Oakengates, Madeley** and **Dawley** were among the towns to be incorporated, and the name chosen in the 1960s commemorates Thomas Telford, whose influence can be seen all over the county. Thomas Telford was a Scot, born in Eskdale in 1757, who came to Shrewsbury in 1786. Appointed County Surveyor, he quickly got to work on such enterprises as Shrewsbury jail, Bridgnorth, a host of bridges, an Aqueduct, canals and the Holyhead Road. He designed distinctive milestones for the road, one of which is now at the Blists Hill Museum. Telford's many ambitious developments include the huge (450-acre) Town Park, with nature trails, sports fields, lakes, gardens and play areas. Wonderland is an enchanting and enchanted woodland whose fairytale attractions include Snow White's Cottage, the Three Little Pigs and the Wrekin Giant. On the northern outskirts, at Preston-on-the-Weald Moor, is **Hoo Farm Animal Kingdom**, which numbers among its inhabitants ostriches, chipmunks, deer and llamas. Events include

Sheep Steeplechase, Hoo Farm Animal Kingdom

lamb feeding, milking and the famous sheep steeplechase. Christmas brings Santa and his animals to the magic grotto. Tel: 01952 677917

Telford Steam Railway Trust keeps a number of old locomotives, some of them ex-GWR, in working condition at the old shed and yard at Horsehay.

AROUND TELFORD

OAKENGATES   Map 3 ref F5
2 miles NE of Telford on the A5

Oakengates, on the eastern edge of the metropolis of Telford, is the birthplace of Sir Gordon Richards, perhaps the greatest jockey this country has ever produced. His father was a miner and the young Gordon first learned to ride on pit ponies. When he retired from the saddle, he had ridden 4,872 winners and was champion jockey for 20 years. Frankie and Kieren have a long way to go!

Sean Jones has practised his culinary skills in some of the top restaurants in the UK and France, and now it is the turn of Shropshire to enjoy his fine cooking in the art nouveau-themed surroundings of **Browsers Restaurant** at Oakengates in the purlieus of Telford (five minutes from the M54 and A5). Care and passion go into every dish on the internationally inspired à la carte menu, which typically runs from Thai spinach soup and a paté of pork, apple and

Browsers Restaurant, 25 Market Street, Oakengates, Telford, Shropshire TF2 6EL. Tel: 01952 612880 Fax: 01952 616646

calvados to sea bass with an orange and basil butter sauce, breast of guinea fowl filled with a wild mushroom and herb mousse, and fillet of lamb with marsala sauce served on a bed of red cabbage. Lynn Jones runs front of house in friendly fashion, and on certain evenings a very special ambience and style are created when live music accompanies the excellent food and drink. Open Wednesday to Saturday evenings and Sunday lunchtime.

Owner John Ellis's expertise in real ales has helped the **Crown Inn** to become a real mecca for lovers of the traditional brew. Up to ten real ales, many

Crown Inn, Market Street, Oakengates, Telford, Shropshire TF2 6EA
Tel: 01952 610888 web: www.oakengates.com

from local independent brewers, are available at this grand old pub (first licensed in 1835), which John took over in 1995. He took great care to retain the character and ambience, and the traditional furnishings in the bars are complemented by prints of old transport scenes and a collection of vintage beer mats and posters. The pub holds beer festivals on the first weekends of May and October, using an amazing 29 handpulls, and was runner-up in the Cask Ale Pub of the Year competition in 1998 and again in 1999. Malt whiskies are another speciality, with around 16 varieties on sale. Solid nourishment is provided by filled rolls served Monday to Friday lunchtimes. Thursday nights are music nights, including regular audition nights when first-timers can take the mike for their 15 minutes of fame. The celebrated Oakengates Theatre is 100 yards down the road.

KETLEY   Map 3 ref F4
2 miles N of Telford on the A518

On the A518 in one of the five towns that make up the metropolis of Telford, **The Wrens Nest** offers a warm welcome from friendly tenants Mike and Edith Lynall and their daughter-in-law Debbie, who is the chef. The comfortable lounge bar of this modern pub is hung with prints of the locality, while behind the bar is an impressive collection of gnomes (101 at the last count!). There's plenty of variety on Debbie's weekly changing menu, from jacket potatoes with a choice of 10 fillings to lasagne, liver and bacon casserole, steaks, scampi, trout and

The Wrens Nest, Ketley, Near Telford, Shropshire TF1 4HJ
Tel: 01952 244851

vegetarian dishes. "Seniors lunches" are a very popular feature. A really likeable place, and an ideal lunch stop for motorists.

SHIFNAL

MAP 3 REF F5

2 miles E of Telford on the A464

Once a staging post on the Holyhead Road, Shifnal has an unexpectedly large church with a Norman chancel arch, a carved Italian pulpit and an Italian reredos. New owners Aled and Debbie Rees have made **Jaspers** the most popular place for a meal in Shifnal. A free house, bistro and restaurant, it stands on the

Jaspers, Victoria Road, Shifnal, Shropshire TF11 8AF
Tel: 01952 460452

A464 close to the centre of a town that was once a stop on the London-Holyhead coaching route. The building dates from 1830, and original beams are a feature in the lounge. There are two main eating areas, a 36-seat restaurant and a 30-seat bistro decorated by Aled and Debbie in cheerful Mediterranean style. A full selection of bar meals is served at lunchtime, with Bookmaker's Sandwich (rump steak in a baguette) among the favourites. The imaginative, well-priced main menus are supplemented by a specials board that includes fresh fish and vegetarian dishes. In the old days Jaspers was called The Union and brewed some of the strongest beer in England. It now offers an impressive range of real ales, plus cider from Herefordshire, and excellent house wines on an extensive list. The name Jaspers remembers a waiter who stayed on after his death to haunt the cellar! In addition to the inside seating, tables are set outside on a paved area at the front and in the garden at the back.

On the A41, at **Cosford** near Shifnal, the **RAF Museum** is home to an important collection of aircraft, aero engines and missiles from all over the world. Classic British airliners like the Comet, Britannia, Viscount and VC10 share space with warplanes such as the Spitfire, Mosquito, Lincoln and Liberator. The missile collection, numbering over 40, charts the development of these weapons of war from the 1920s to the present time. Tel: 01902 376200

TONG   MAP 3 REF G5
5 miles E of Telford on the A41

Tong is an attractive village which once had a castle, founded, according to legend, by the wizard Merlin. Where was he when the castle was blown up in 1954? The Vernons and the Durants were the Lords of the Manor in Tong for many years and they are commemorated in 15th-century **Church of St Bartholomew**. The Vernons were a particularly distinguished lot: one was a Speaker of the House of Commons and another was Lord High Constable to Henry V. In the Golden Chapel, which has a superb gilded, fan-vaulted ceiling, there is a bust of Arthur Vernon, who was a don at Cambridge University. Venetia Stanley, descended from the Vernons and the Earls of Derby, was a famed beauty who was lauded by poets and artists. She counted Ben Jonson, Van Dyck and the Earl of Dorset among her lovers, but in 1625 she made the unfortunate move of marrying Sir Kenelm Digby, whose father had been executed for his part in the Gunpowder Plot. She died tragically young, some say at the hands of her jealous husband.

Charles Dickens is thought to have had Tong in mind when he wrote *The Old Curiosity Shop*: Little Nell's home was right by the church, and some say that she is buried in the churchyard.

A couple of miles east of Tong is **White Ladies Priory**, where the ruins of a 12th-century church may be seen.

GREAT CHATWELL
6 miles E of Telford off the A41

MAP 3 REF G4

Narrow roads lead from the A41 south of Newport to the unspoilt village of Great Chatwell and **The Red Lion**, a delightful creeper-clad pub with family owners Pamela and Mike Smith. The two original 17th century rooms have been extended to create a new lounge and a 50-cover dining room, where two chefs provide visitors with an extensive choice of starters, main courses (includ-

**The Red Lion Inn, Great Chatwell, Near Newport, Shropshire TF10 9BJ
Tel: 01952 691366**

ing vegetarian options) and all-time English favourites among the puds. There's also a children's menu, making the pub a popular choice with young families, and a less formal menu of bar snacks. To accompany the food, or to enjoy on their own, are a good selection of real ales including two guest ales each month, and a reasonably priced list of wines. Another attraction, particularly for families, is the garden, where, when the weather allows, food and drink can be enjoyed at picnic-style tables, and where a play area, two aviaries and a miniature pony are guaranteed to keep the children happy.

BOSCOBEL
7 miles E of Telford off the A41

MAP 3 REF G5

After Charles ll was defeated by the Roundheads at the Battle of Worcester in 1651, he fled for his life and was advised to seek refuge in a remote hunting lodge called **Boscobel House**, already known as a safe house for royals on the run. By day the King hid in the branches of an old oak tree, while at night he would creep into the house and hide in secret rooms with one of his trusty officers. He eventually escaped, of course, and nine years later was restored to the throne. The house has changed considerably since Charles's time, but it's still full of atmosphere and interest, with an exhibition giving a vivid account of the King's adventures. Every visitor naturally wants to see the famous oak in which he hid, but it is no longer standing, destroyed by souvenir-hunting loyalists. Today there stands a descendant of the original, itself now more than 300 years old.

NEWPORT
MAP 3 REF F4

6 miles NE of Telford off the A41

A handsome town which lost many of its buildings in a fire in 1665. Most of the buildings on the broad main street are Georgian or early Victorian. There's plenty to keep the visitor active in the area, including the **Lilleshall National Sports Centre** and the ruins of Lilleshall Abbey, the extensive and evocative remains of an Augustinian abbey.

WESTON-UNDER-LIZARD
MAP 3 REF G5

5 miles E of Telford on the A5

Just over the border into Staffordshire stands **Weston Park**, a fine restoration mansion that has been the home of the Earls of Bradford for 15 generations. It was recently chosen by the Prime Minister for the Retreat Day of the G8 Summit of World Leaders. Inside, they would have admired a wealth of treasures including paintings by Van Dyck, Gainsborough and Stubbs, fine books, porcelain and Beauvais and Gobelin tapestries. The setting of 1,000 acres of Capability Brown landscape embraces a deer park, pets corner and playground with a miniature railway. Lots of special events take place each year. Tel: 01952 850207

TELFORD TO SHREWSBURY

WELLINGTON
MAP 3 REF F5

1 mile NE of Telford on the A442

Wellington is part of the new town of Telford but still retains much of its Victorian look. The Church of All Saints is the work of George Steuart, better known for St Chad's in Shrewsbury. A new attraction in town is the National Trust's **Sunnycroft**, a late-Victorian gentleman's suburban villa typical of the kind that were built for wealthy business and professional men. The house and its contents are largely unaltered, and in the grounds are pig sties, a kitchen garden, orchards, a conservatory and a Wellingtonia avenue. Tel: 0870 6081259.

Flapjacks, 4a Bell Street, Wellington, Shropshire TF1 1LS Tel: 01952 270276

In a market town of many attractions, **Flapjacks** is a real gem, and a recent survey of Shropshire residents nominated it as the premier tea room in the area. It is a focal point for many Wellingtonians for morning coffee, lunch and afternoon tea, tempting with superb home-baked cakes and savoury dishes to be enjoyed in a cosy beamed room hung with the work of local artists. Sandwiches, plain or toasted, make satisfying quick snacks, and all-day breakfasts are joined at lunchtime by daily specials such as nut roast or lasagne. Flapjacks is unlicensed, but has a selection of teas, filter coffee and soft drinks. Full waiter service adds a further touch of distinction to this splendid little place, which is open from 10 till 4 Tuesday to Saturday.

A couple of miles north of Wellington, at **Longdon-on-Tern**, stands the **aqueduct** built by Thomas Telford as a pilot for other, better-known constructions.

South of here, on the other side of the M54/A5, is one of the best-known landmarks in the whole country. **The Wrekin**, which reaches up over 1,300 feet, is the site of a prehistoric hill fort, visible for many miles around and accessible by a network of public footpaths. The reward for reaching the top is beautiful panoramic views across to the neighbouring counties. In Roman times it was used as a base by the Cornovii tribe before they were moved to Viroconium. Shropshire folklore tells us that it was 'put' there by a malicious giant who was carrying a huge load of earth to dam the Severn and flood Shrewsbury, simply because he didn't like the people. The giant met a cobbler, who persuaded him against this evil act, whereupon the giant dropped the load he was carrying - and that's The Wrekin.

WROXETER
7 miles W of Telford on the B4380

MAP 2 REF E5

In the village of Wroxeter, beside the B4380, is one of the most important Roman sites ever brought to light. *Viroconium* was the first town to be established by the Romans in this part of the country and developed from being a military settlement to a sizeable civilian town where the Cornovii tribe were settled. It's an absolutely fascinating place, where the highlights include extensive remains of a 2nd-century bathhouse complex. Some of the major excavated items are on display here, many more at **Rowley's House Museum** in Shrewsbury. Also in the village is Wroxeter Roman Vineyard (Tel: 01743 761888), where there is not only a vineyard producing both red and white wines but additional delights in the shape of rare-breed animals and a lavender field.

ATCHAM   MAP 2 REF E5
7 miles W of Telford on the B4380

The village stands at the point where the Severn is crossed by the Roman road. The splendid old seven-arched bridge is now redundant, having been replaced by a new neighbour some time ago, but is still in situ. The old bridge was designed by John Gwynne, who was a founder member of the Royal Academy and the designer of Magdalen Bridge in Oxford.

Attingham Park, run by the National Trust, is perhaps the finest house in Shropshire, a splendid neo-classical mansion set in 250 delightful acres. Designed by George Steuart for the 1st Lord Berwick, it has the grandest of Regency interiors, ambassadorial silver, Italian furniture and Grand Tour paintings hanging in the John Nash gallery. The tea room is lined with paintings of the 5th Lord Berwick's Herefordshire cattle. Humphrey Repton landscaped the park, where visitors can enjoy woodland and riverside walks and see the deer. Tel: 01743 709203.

Attingham Home Farm (Tel: 01743 709243), the original home farm of the grand house, comprises buildings dating mainly from about 1800, and the yard retains the atmosphere of a traditional Shropshire farm. Many breeds of farm animals are represented: pigs - Oxford, Sandy, Iron Age, Vietnamese pot-bellied; sheep - Jacob, Shetland and Ryeland; cattle - Jerseys, Longhair, Dexter, Red Poll, British White. The rabbit house is particularly popular with youngsters, and there are usually some orphaned lambs for children to bottle-feed.

SHREWSBURY

The River Severn winds round the lovely county town in a horseshoe bend, making it almost an island site, and it was on two hills within this protected site that the Saxon town developed. The Normans under Roger de Montgomery took over after the conquest, building the castle and the great Benedictine abbey. In the 15th and 16th centuries Shrewsbury prospered through the wool trade, and evidence of its affluence shows in the many black-and-white timbered buildings that still line the streets. In Victorian times steam made Shrewsbury an important railway centre whilst at the same time Darwin, born

Charles Darwin Statue, Shrewsbury

and educated in the town, was rocking the world with his theories. Everywhere there is a sense of history, and the Museums do a particularly fine job of bringing the past to life, in terms of both human and natural history. **Rowley's House** is a glorious timber-framed building of the late 16th century, with an adjoining brick and stone mansion of 1618. The home of William Rowley, 17th-century draper, brewer and leading citizen, now contains an impressive collection of pieces from Viroconium, along with spectacular displays of costumes, natural history and geology. Tel: 01743 361196. A short walk away is **Clive House**, in the Georgian area of the town. Clive of India live here in 1762 while he was Mayor, and one or two mementoes can be seen. The major displays are of Shropshire ceramics and the life of Charles Darwin, whose statue stands opposite the Castle. Tel: 01743 354811. The Castle, dating from 1083, was built by the Norman Earl Roger de Montgomery and last saw action in the Civil War. It was converted by Thomas Telford into a private residence and now houses the **Shropshire Regimental Museum** with the collections of the Kings Shropshire Yeomanry Cavalry and the Shropshire Royal Horse Artillery. Tel: 01743 358516.

A museum with a difference is **Coleham Pumping Station** at **Longden Coleham** (Tel: 01743 362947), which houses the splendid Renshaw pumping engines that powered Shrewsbury's sewerage system until 1970.

The Abbey, like the Castle, was founded by Roger de Montgomery, on the site of a Saxon wooden church. In 1283 a parliament met in the Chapter House, the first national assembly in which the Commons were involved. The Abbey Church remains a place of worship, and in 1997 a stained glass window depicting St Benedict was dedicated to the memory of Edith Pargeter. This lady, writing under the name of Ellis Peters, created the character of Brother Cadfael, who lived at the Abbey and became one of the country's best-loved fictional characters when portrayed by Derek Jacobi in the television series. Hard by the Abbey, **The Shrewsbury Quest** (Tel: 01743 243324) presents the sights and sounds of medieval Shrewsbury. Visitors can see Brother Cadfael's workshop, solve mysteries, create their own medieval manuscripts and breathe in the fragrance of a monastic herb garden. Complementing the town's Museum and Archaeological Services, a Records and Research Service was opened in a new building in 1995.

It has 5 ½ miles of material relating to Shropshire past and present, including many original records and extensive microfilm records. Shrewsbury has more than 30 churches and among the finest are St Mary's and St Chad's. **St Mary's**, the town's only complete medieval church, originated in the late Saxon period, but the earliest features of the present building are of the 12th century. The stained glass, monuments and fittings are quite out of the ordinary, and the spire has claims to being the third highest in the land. One of the memorials is to Admiral Benbow, a national hero who died in 1702 and is also remembered in innumerable pub signs. **St Chad's** is the work of Attingham Hall's designer George Steuart, who was commissioned to design a replacement for the original, which fell down in 1788. His church is very unusual in having a circular nave.

Guided tours and suggested walks cover all aspects of this marvellous town, including a **Brother Cadfael tour** and walks in the beautiful countryside that is all around. One walk takes in the spot to the north of town now known as **Battlefield**, where in 1403 the armies of Henry IV and the insurgent Harry Percy (Harry Hotspur) met. 50,000 men were deployed in all, and in the brief but bloody battle Hotspur was among the many casualties. A church was built near the mass grave, where 1,600 bodies are buried, a monument to the fallen and also an oasis of wildlife in the town environment.

The Bell Inn was built in the 18th century and became a public house in the 19th, and its bars, where traditional pub games are still played, have the warm, cosy appeal of days gone by. Sue and George Lewis, owners since 1997, have

The Bell Inn, Wenlock Road, Cross Houses, Near Shrewsbury, Shropshire SY5 6JJ Tel: 01743 761264

long experience in the licensed trade, and put out the welcome mat for all visitors, whether the visit is for a drink, a meal or to stay in one of the three well-appointed en suite bedrooms - one family room, one double room and one twin room. The pub is set in an acre of grounds, with a beer garden, ample parking and hanging baskets that have won prizes for their colourful displays. The pub is open (and food served) all day Wednesday, Friday, Saturday and Sunday, lunchtime and evenings Monday and Thursday, and evenings only on Tuesday. The menu provides plenty of variety, with 'summertime specials' a popular feature. The inn lies four miles southeast of Shrewsbury on the A458, well placed for exploring this delightful area.

For more than 20 years Pat and Alan Bell have been greeting guests at their large early-Victorian family home in a secluded setting on the southern out-skirts of Shrewsbury off the A49. The atmosphere at **Moneybrook Guest House** is friendly and relaxing; in the summer the tree-shaded grounds provide a per-

Moneybrook Guest House, Hereford Road, Meole Brace, Shrewsbury, Shropshire SY3 9LB Tel: 01743 355559 Fax: 01743 343262

fect spot for afternoon tea, while in cooler months the cosy guest lounge offers warmth and comfort in abundance. The four non-smoking bedrooms - single, double, twin and family room - are well decorated and comfortably furnished; all have washbasins, colour TV and tea-making equipment. A full English break-fast is served, with evening meals by prior arrangement. Ample parking.

Shrewsbury Flower Show is Britain's best two-day summer show and each August for more than a century the show has been held in the picturesque setting of **Quarry Park**. Three million blooms fill three giant marquees, and the show includes a musical programme and fireworks displays. Make a note of the 2000 event - it's August 11 and 12.

AROUND SHREWSBURY

WITHINGTON
MAP 2 REF E4

3 miles E of Shrewsbury off the B4394

A warm welcome is guaranteed from Janice Buswell at the **Hare & Hounds**, which lies at the heart of a village three miles east of Shrewsbury. Born locally, Janice has 25 years experience in the licensed trade, and her pub is the focal point of village social life, with darts and dominoes teams and a large beer garden used in summer for the village fete and other celebrations. The roomy bar is traditional in style, with oak-beamed ceiling and coal fire, while outside, hanging baskets and flower tubs bring a blaze of colour in spring and summer; the patio is a real sun trap. Reached off the B4394 or B5062, and only a short drive from J7 of the M54.

The Hare & Hounds, Walcot Road, Withington, Near Shrewsbury, Shropshire SY4 4PY Tel: 01743 709446

FITZ

MAP 2 REF D4

4 miles NW of Shrewsbury off the B5067

Dawn and Neil Baly welcome guests from all over the world to **Fitz Manor**, an Elizabethan manor house built in 1450 and half-timbered in typical Shropshire style. Fitz is a tiny, unspoilt hamlet off the B5067, as peaceful and tranquil as

**Fitz Manor, Fitz, Bomere Heath, Near Shrewsbury, Shropshire SY4 3AS
Tel: 01743 850295**

anyone could want, but only 15 minutes by car from Shrewsbury. The interior of the home is an intriguing delight, especially the candle-lit dining room and the oak-panelled sitting room. There are three guest bedrooms - a double, a twin and a single - which share a bathroom; however, a private bathroom can be made available by arrangement. Fitz Manor has a beautiful garden full of herbaceous borders, secret paces, a swimming pool and an abundance of fruit and vegetables. There are also tracks through woods leading down to the River Severn where guests can stroll at leisure. This is very much a family home and Dawn and Neil enjoy treating their guests as friends and usually sit down to dinner with them. Open all year.

WOLLASTON

MAP 2 REF C5

8 miles W of Shrewsbury on the A458

The church here has a memorial to Thomas Parr, widely claimed to be the long-est-lived Englishman, dying at the ripe old age of 152. He lived through ten reigns, married for the first time at 88, raised a family and married again at 122. He is buried in Westminster Abbey, so someone must have believed his story.

WESTBURY
MAP 2 REF C5

9 miles W of Shrewsbury on the B4387

Massive earthworks are all that remain of **Caus Castle**, built in Norman times by the FitzCorbets.

The quiet atmosphere of a comfortable family home brings a wide variety of guests to Carol Yarwood's **Station Lodge**, which was built in 1899 as a hotel for the passing railway trade. Closed in 1966, it has been patiently restored by the current owners, keeping the character and adding much interior interest. There are three spacious guest bedrooms - two doubles and a twin - appointed in traditional style and enhanced with personal touches. A full English breakfast is

Station Lodge, Westbury, Near Shrewsbury, Shropshire SY5 9DA
Tel: 01743 884331

served, with other choices available, and a three-course evening meal (prior arrangement only) uses local and organic ingredients as far as possible. Station Lodge lies nine miles west of Shrewsbury on the B4387 in great walking country; the less energetic will be happy strolling around the large garden. ETB 4Diamonds. No smoking.

MONTFORD
MAP 2 REF C4

4 miles W of Shrewsbury off the A5

It's worth pausing at Montford to look at the church where Charles Darwin was buried for a time. His body was subsequently moved to Westminster Abbey, showing that the furore caused by his theories had largely died down soon after his death – but not entirely, as the *The Origin of Species* and *The Descent of Man* can still arouse fierce debate. Just beyond Montford are the ruins of Shrawardine Castle.

MELVERLEY
MAP 2 REF C4

10 miles W of Shrewsbury off the B4393

Country lanes lead to the remarkable **Church of St Peter**, which stands serenely, if somewhat precariously, on the banks of the River Vyrnwy. This is a most unusual church: built in 1406 after the original was destroyed by Owen Glendower, it is timber-framed and painted black and white inside and out.

NESSCLIFFE
MAP 2 REF C4

9 miles NW of Shrewsbury on the A5

Near the village of Nesscliffe, which lies halfway between Shrewsbury and Oswestry, is **Nesscliffe Hill Country Park**, where paths lead up through woodland to the summit and fine views over Shropshire. The Hill is a sandstone escarpment, popular for walking and rock climbing; cut into the face of an abandoned quarry are caves, one of them reputedly the lair of the 16th-century worthy-turned-highwayman Humphrey Kynaston. The whole area southwest of Oswestry, including Nesscliffe, Knockin, Ruyton and Melverley, is known as Kynaston Country.

A short distance north of Nesscliffe, on the B4397, is the village of **Ruyton-XI-Towns**, which acquired its unusual name in medieval times when 11 communities were united into the borough of Ruyton.

8 North Shropshire

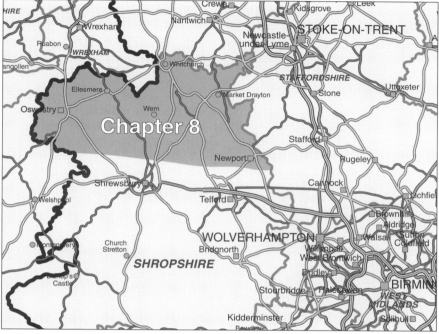

Our journey ends in the northern part of Shropshire, which includes the historic town of Oswestry and the county's own Lake District around Ellesmere.

OSWESTRY

Close to the Welsh border, Oswestry is an important market town whose look is mainly Georgian and Victorian, due in part to the fires which regularly ravaged timber-framed buildings. The town grew up around **St Oswald's Well**. Oswald was a Saxon king who was killed in a battle in 642 against a rival Saxon king, Penda of Mercia. Oswald's body was dismembered and hung on the branches of a tree. An eagle swooped and carried off one of his arms and where the limb fell to the ground a spring bubbled up to mark the spot. Thus St Oswald's Well came into being, soon to become a place of pilgrimage renowned for its healing powers.

There are many fine old buildings in Oswestry, none finer than the **Church of St Oswald**. It played an important part in the Civil War, when it was used as an observation point during the siege of the town by the Parliamentarians. The oldest section is the tower, which dates back to around 1200. The interior is beautiful, and among the treasures are a font presented by Colonel Lloyd of Llanforda as a thanksgiving for the restoration of the monarchy, a Gilbert Scott war memorial and a memorial to Hugh Yale, a member of the family that founded Yale University.

Standing in the grounds of the church is the 15th-century **Holbache House**. Once a grammar school, this handsome building now houses the Tourist Information Centre and the **Heritage Centre** (Tel: 01691 662753), with displays of local interest and exhibitions of arts and crafts. Ferrequinologists (railway buffs)

Oswestry Heritage & Exhibition Centre

will make tracks for the **Cambrian Museum of Transport** on Oswald Road (Tel: 01691 671749). Oswestry was the headquarters of the Cambrian Railway Company until it amalgamated with the GWR in 1922, and as late as the 1960s there were over 1,000 railwaymen in the area. Locomotives, carriages and wagons have been built and repaired in Oswestry for over 100 years, and the mainte-

Oswestry Light Railway

nance of 300 miles of track was directed from offices in the station building. One of the old engine sheds now houses a small museum with a collection of railway memorabilia and also some old bicycles and motorbikes. One of the locomotives is regularly steamed up by the volunteers of the Cambrian Railway Society.

In 1559 a plague killed almost a third of the town's population and the **Croeswylan Stone** commemorates this disaster, marking the spot to which the market was moved during the plague. It is sometimes referred to as the Cross of Weeping.

Food and hospitality share top billing at **Bromley's 'Hide Away'**, a charming tea room-café in traditional style, tucked away in the centre of town. The premises, originally a warehouse, were run as a café by the Bromley family for many years, and Carol and Brian Sutton, taking over in early 1999, have quickly made their mark. All the sweets and the majority of the main courses are home-made, and on Wednesday and Friday there's a special dish of the day. Freshly baked scones with jam or cream and made-to-order sandwiches are popular light snacks, accompanied by a hot or cold beverage (the café is unlicensed), while among the main courses

Bromley's 'Hide Away', 3a Willow Street, Oswestry, Shropshire SY11 1AF Tel: 01691 652350

steak pie, home-cooked ham, fillet of plaice and variations on the good old English breakfast are among the favourite orders. Fruit pies (cherry, apple, apricot or blackcurrant), served with cream, ice cream or custard, round off a meal in fine style. Open 9-3 Tuesday-Saturday. Seats for 50; children welcome.

Behind a handsome stone facade with an ecclesiastical look (it was actually a Victorian school), **The Walls** is a restaurant and wine bar of immense appeal, certainly one of the best places for many miles around to enjoy a good meal in convivial surroundings. Under the beams in the brick-walled main dining area visitors will find an unfussy, unpretentious atmosphere assisted by friendly, thoughtful staff, good food and wines and, on Sunday, an extravagant buffet lunch that brings back memories of what the great tradition of British Sunday lunch should be. Starters on a typical à la carte menu are often just that little bit different, perhaps smoked salmon soup flavoured with fennel and sorrel, or goose rillettes with kumquat marmalade; and main courses run from Ceiriog trout served simply with a herby mayonnaise through pork belly with beans to ostrich steak, pasta arrabbiata with toasted goat's cheese and British beef steak,

The Walls, Welsh Walls, Oswestry, Shropshire SY11 1AW
Tel: 01691 670970 Fax: 01691 653820

hung for a minimum of three weeks and served au poivre, with Café de Paris sauce or with Roquefort and red wine sauce. There are well over 200 references on a wine list that is clearly the work of a true enthusiast in owner-chef Geoffrey Hughes - expertly compiled and absolutely full of variety and interest. The setting is perfect for parties of all kinds, lectures, craft fairs and wine tastings, and is also increasingly in demand for marriage ceremonies and celebrations. Opening times are 10.30am till late Monday-Saturday, lunch only (last orders 2.30) on Sunday.

The Greyhound is a family concern par excellence, with Bob and Barbara Berkett joined by Pauline and Brian and Sue and Paul. The inn occupies a prominent corner spot just moments from the centre of town on the road to Llansilin, and started life as a coaching stop with stabling. Overnight accommodation is provided in four first-rate bedrooms, two of them en suite, all well decorated

The Greyhound Inn, Willow Street, Oswestry, Shropshire SY11 1AJ
Tel: 01691 653837

and furnished, with everything necessary for a comfortable stay. The Greyhound is a wet house (no food served) except for residents' breakfasts, and in the bar and lounge a good selection of beers keeps thirsts in check. The pub has a smashing garden and courtyard at the back, and a large car park.

On the northern edge of town, **Old Oswestry** is an impressive example of an Iron Age fortress, first occupied in about 300BC. It was on the border of the territory held by the Cornovii and is one of several in the region. At the southwest corner of the fort can be seen **Wat's Dyke**, built at the same time and for the same purpose – delineating the border between Saxon Mercia and the Welsh – as the better-known Offa's Dyke. Who was Wat? We know not, but he could have been one of Offa's officers.

AROUND OSWESTRY

MAESBURY
Map 2 ref C3

2 miles S of Oswestry off the A5 or A483

The village was one of the main transit points on the **Montgomery Canal**, and many of the canal buildings at **Maesbury Marsh** are still standing, along with some boatmen's cottages.

Easily found near the little school on the edge of Maesbury village, **Ashfield Farmhouse** offers high-class bed and breakfast accommodation, a quiet, relaxed atmosphere and a warm and friendly welcome from Margaret and David Jones. Their lovely old house, parts of which trace back to the 16th century, was once a coach house and later a Georgian farmhouse, and was at the heart of a working farm when they bought it in the 1970s. The three upstairs letting bedrooms offer en suite or private shower/bathrooms, and one double has an adjoining room that's perfect for families. Colour TV, beverage tray, hairdryer, clock radio, electric fan and central heating are standard features, and the cosy, old-fashioned drawing room has a good selection of books and games for whiling away the odd hour. The setting, in large gardens with an orchard, is both beautiful and peaceful, and there are splendid views of the Welsh mountains and the

Ashfield Farmhouse, Maesbury, Near Oswestry, Shropshire SY10 8JH
Tel & Fax: 01691 653589

rolling Shropshire hills. The garden is an ideal spot for afternoon tea, and packed lunches can be made up for guests exploring this picturesque part of the country. No evening meals are served, but good cheer is available at the excellent village inn just a short walk away. The farmhouse has plenty of safe parking and there are lockable old stables for pets, bicycles, and other valuables. Maesbury lies a mile south of the edge of Oswestry before Maesbury Marsh. It's also only a mile from the A5 and A483.

Immediately south of Maesbury Marsh is the village of **Woolston**, where **St Winifred's Well** is said to have been a resting place for saints' bones being carried to their final destinations.

KNOCKIN
Map 2 ref C4
5 miles S of Oswestry on the B4396

In a pleasant village with an interesting church and a motte, **The Old Forge** is a top-of-the-range bed and breakfast establishment with a QQQQ AA classification. Christine and Bob Goss run what was once, as it name suggests, the village forge, some of whose associated buildings date back to 1600. Christine was adjudged among the top 20 hosts by the AA in 1998, and this charming place has three outstanding guest rooms, two, both en suite, in the main house, and the other in a splendidly renovated outbuilding. This room, with beams and a great deal of character, is at ground level and has its own patio where guests can take the sun or even enjoy an alfresco breakfast. (Evening meals are not served, but good food and drink are provided at the neighbouring inn.) The Old Forge lies five miles south of Oswestry on the B4396. Children are welcome, and cots can be made available. No smoking.

The Old Forge, Knockin, Near Oswestry, Shropshire SY10 8HJ
Tel: 01691 682394 Fax: 01691 682423

LLANYMYNECH
MAP 2 REF B4

7 miles S of Oswestry on the A483

A small diversion is well worth while to visit Llanymynech, once a town of some standing, with a major canal and a thriving industry based on limestone. It was also a railway junction. The **Llanymynech Hills**, which include a section of **Offa's Dyke**, make for good walking, with the old limestone workings to add interest – you can still see the old bottle lime kilns and an unusual Hoffman rotary kiln. The quarried limestone was taken to the kilns on a tramway and, after processing, to the nearby canalside wharf. Part of the quarry is now a designated nature reserve and supports abundant bird life. On top of the hill are traces of an ancient hill fort.

The **Montgomery Canal** was built at the end of the 18th century mainly for the transportation of limestone from the Llanymynech quarries. Large sections of it are now unnavigable, indeed dry, but a restoration project is under way with the aim of opening 35 miles of waterway from Oswestry through Welshpool to Newtown. Until the boats return there are some delightful walks along the towpath, as well as fishing where it is possible.

WHITTINGTON
MAP 2 REF C3

2 miles E of Oswestry on the A495

On the eastern edge of Oswestry, Whittington once had a castle, but little now remains. Close by is the parish church, where William Walsham How, later Bishop of Wakefield, was the incumbent for almost 30 years. He was a hymnwriter of some standing, one of finest hymns being *For All the Saints*. Dick Whittington may or may not have been born here, but someone who definitely lived at nearby **Halston Hall** for many years was Mad Jack Mytton, whom we met in an earlier chapter.

Park Hall Farm Museum houses a splendid display of 19th-century farm implements and is also home to some rare breed animals and some marvellous Shire horses, who work on the land at certain times. Tel: 01691 652175.

ELLESMERE
MAP 2 REF C3

8 miles E of Oswestry on the A495

The centre of Shropshire's Lakeland, Ellesmere is a pretty market town with Tudor, Georgian and Victorian buildings. The **Old Town Hall** and the **Old Railway Station** are two of the most impressive buildings, but nothing except the mound remains of the castle. The most impressive of all is the parish church of St Mary the Virgin, built by the Knights of St John. It is particularly beautiful inside, with an exceptional 15th-century carved roof in the chapel.

The church overlooks **The Mere**, largest of several lakes that are an equal delight to boating enthusiasts, anglers and birdwatchers. Herons, Canada geese and swans are among the inhabitants of The Mere.

Ellesmere

A mile or so east of Ellesmere, on the A495, is **Welshampton**, whose church was built by Sir George Gilbert Scott in 1863. One of its memorial windows is dedicated to a Basuto chieftain; he had been a student of theology at Canterbury and part of his studies brought him to Welshampton, where he lodged with the vicar. Unfortunately he fell ill and died in the same year that saw the completion of the church.

LLANRHAEADR-YM-MOCHNANT   MAP 2 REF A3
10 miles W of Oswestry on the B4580

Llanrhaeadr is actually well over the border into Wales, but it's well worth the ten-mile drive west along the B4580 from Oswestry to sample the delights of **The Three Tuns**. In a picturesque village setting, the pub is owned and run by Barbie Roberts and her son Simon, and the place has an abundance of old-fashioned charm, with half-panelled walls, an inglenook fireplace and a quarry-tiled floor. Barbie, with the able assistance of Viv and Amanda, keeps visitors happy with her top-quality home-cooked food, served lunchtime and evening in the summer and at weekends in the winter; children are welcome until early evening. There's a separate games room, and to the rear a small, well-

**The Three Tuns, Llanrhaeadr-ym-Mochnant, Near Oswestry,
Powys SY10 0JU Tel: 01691 780263**

kept walled garden where you can take your victuals on fine days. As we went to press (summer 1999) plans were afoot to make overnight accommodation available.

MARKET DRAYTON

Market Drayton was mentioned in the Domesday Book as Magna Draitune. It changed its name when Abbot Simon Combermere obtained a Royal Market Charter in 1245:

"Know that we have granted and by this our present charter confirmed to Brother Simon Abbot of Combermere and the minks serving God there that they and their successors forever shall have a weekly market in their manor of Drayton on Wednesday."

And so they have, every Wednesday.

The fire of 1651 raised most of the town, so there is now quite a diversity of styles among the buildings. One of the most interesting is the **Buttercross**, built in 1842 to enable farmers' wives to display their wares protected from the weather. The crest it carries is of the Corbet family, Lords of the Manor since 1650.

Market Drayton is often referred to as 'The Home of the Gingerbread'. Gingerbread has been baked here for 200 years and is made in all shapes and sizes, the best known being the Gingerbread Man. Traditionally dunked in port, it's

Market Drayton

also very good to nibble on the **Discovery Trail** that takes in the sights of the town. Gingerbread dates back far more than 200 years, of course, and Shakespeare had a good word for it:

> *"An' I had but one penny in the world*
> *thou shouldst have it to buy gingerbread."*

Market Drayton's most famous son (actually born just outside) was Clive of India, whose childhood escapades in the town included climbing the church tower and sitting on one of the gargoyles, and building a dam to flood a shop whose owner was unwilling to pay protection money.

AROUND MARKET DRAYTON

MORETON SAY
Map 3 ref E3

3 miles W of Market Drayton on the A41

Clive of India is buried in a simple grave in the churchyard, with an equally modest memorial in the church itself.

HODNET
Map 3 ref E3

4 miles SW of Market Drayton on the A53

The sizeable village of Hodnet is overlooked by the church of St Luke from its hilltop position. The church is Norman, with some unusual features including a christening gate and wedding steps, and it has a very distinctive octagonal tower. There are some ornate carvings around the 17th-century font, and a chapel is dedicated to the Heber-Percy family, owners of **Hodnet Hall**. The most illustrious member of the family was Bishop Heber, who wrote, among many other hymns, *From Greenland's Icy Mountains*. Hodnet Hall is an Elizabethan-style mansion built in the 1870s, but the real reason for a visit here is the wonderful gardens, which extend over 60 acres and were carefully planted (Brigadier Heber-Percy masterminded the transformation) to provide a show of colour throughout the seasons. Tel: 01630 685202.

MARCHAMLEY
Map 3 ref E3

4 miles SW of Market Drayton on the A442

The beautiful Georgian mansion **Hawkestone Hall** was the ancestral home of the Hill family from 1556 until 1906. The Hall is now the seat of a religious order, but the principal rooms, including the splendid Venetian Saloon, are open for a short time in the summer (Tel: 01630 685242). **The Pleasure Gardens** comprise terraces, lily pond, herbaceous borders and extensive woodland. On the same estate, at Weston-under-Lizard, is **Hawkestone Park**, a woodland fantasy of caves and follies and grottoes, of tunnels and secret pathways. The Hills built this extraordinary park, which if it were built today would probably be called a theme park. Tel: 01939 200611.

COLEHURST
Map 3 ref F3

4 miles S of Market Drayton off the A529/A41

In a beautiful and relatively unknown part of England stands an old manor house trapped in a time warp. The owners describe visiting **Old Colehurst Manor** as 'a journey back through time to the real 16th century' and guests down the years are in full agreement. It took seven years to restore the manor to its full glory, during which time it was painstakingly studied, taken apart and rebuilt

**Old Colehurst Manor, Colehurst, Near Market Drayton,
Shropshire TF9 2JB Tel: 01630 638833**

using traditional building and carpentry skills. The result of Bjorn and Maria's efforts and dedication is a truly authentic and historically accurate house. Weddings and period house parties, with old recipes masterminded by Maria, are held at weekends, but B&B guests can appreciate the splendour and the quiet rural surroundings at special rates during the week. Once you come through the oak gates the past comes romantically alive, both in the splendidly appointed bedrooms and day rooms, and in the tranquil grounds, which include walled, rose, herb and knot gardens. The manor and grounds are also open for day visits from the beginning of April to the end of September. The manor is a non-smoking establishment.

NORTON IN HALES
MAP 3 REF F2
3 miles NE of Market Drayton off the A51

Built as a stopping off place for coaches in the early 18th century, **The Hinds Head** stands next to the ancient church in a village three miles north of Market Drayton, signposted off the A529, A51 and B5415. Manager Andrew Hargreaves, with long experience in the trade, knows his customers well, and his hostelry is a favourite spot for visitors wanting to enjoy a high-quality meal in relaxed, hassle-free surroundings. Oak beams, whitewashed walls and a log fire set a

The Hinds Head, Main Road, Norton in Hales, Near Market Drayton, Shropshire TF9 4AT Tel: 01630 653014

traditional scene, and the varied menu relies as much as possible on top-notch locally sourced produce. Meals are served lunchtime and evening Monday to Saturday, and from noon till 6 on Sunday. Weekends are particularly popular, and booking is recommended a fortnight in advance. Ample car parking space.

LOGGERHEADS
Map 3 ref F2

5 miles E of Market Drayton on the A53

Why Loggerheads? No one seems to know the reason for the village to have such a belligerent name. The two establishments featured below seem peaceful enough!

Owners Andrew and Sandra Clinton put years of experience in the licensed trade to good use in running **The Loggerheads**, which stands 5 miles east of Market Drayton at the junction of the A53 and B5026. Behind the ornate facade - whitewashed stone, oak timbers, ornamental carving - the bars, lounge and restaurant are invitingly cosy and comfortable, with beamed ceilings through-out. This is very much the focal point of the village, with a full calendar of social events, and the locals, including the Loggerheads Golfing Society, are joined by many ramblers and tourists, for the village is in a good position for getting to know the scenery and history of the area. Open all year round, the hostelry offers bar snacks and a full restaurant menu lunchtime and evening, and on the night of the new millennium the owners plan a fireworks display and breakfast

**The Loggerheads, Newcastle Road, Loggerheads, Near Market Drayton,
Shropshire TF9 4NX Tel: 01630 672224 Fax: 01630 672080**

at 1.30 am! There's ample parking space, and a beer garden set with tables,
chairs and sunshades.

Visitors to the area looking for a peaceful spot to spend a night or two need
look no further than **Marton**, where Margaret Capper offers comfortable B&B
accommodation in her modern detached house with neat, well-kept gardens.
There are two letting bedrooms, a double with TV, tea-coffee making equipment
and private bathroom, and a single (with an optional extra bed) that's ideal for
children. Sandwiches and evening meals can be arranged with prior notice. No
smoking. No dogs.

**Marton, 7 Broom Hollow, Loggerheads, Near Market Drayton,
Shropshire TF9 4NT Tel: 01630 673329**

WILLOUGHBRIDGE   Map 3 ref G2
6 miles NE of Market Drayton on the A51

Home of the **Dorothy Clive Garden**, with a wide range of specimen and unusual plants. Other attractions are a quarry garden with a spectacular waterfall, flower borders, a scree and water garden. Tel: 01630 647237.

NORTH OF SHREWSBURY

MORETON CORBET   Map 2 ref E4
6 miles N of Shrewsbury on the B5063

Take the A53 to Shawbury and turn left on to the B5063 and you'll soon come across the splendid ruins of **Moreton Corbet Castle**, seat of the local bigwig family. Its stark greystone walls are an entrancing and moving sight, and not at all like a castle. In fact, what remains is the shell of a grand Italian-influenced mansion which was never completed (Corbet funds ran out) and was severely damaged in the Civil War.

PRESTON BROCKHURST   Map 2 ref E3
8 miles N of Shrewsbury on the A49

The village is very close to **Moreton Corbet Castle** and also to **Corbet Wood** and the quarries at Grinshill, which has a notable Victorian church. **Grove Farm** is a 17th-century house, pebbledashed over brick and timber, set in attractive

Grove Farm, Preston Brockhurst, Near Shrewsbury, Shropshire SY4 5QA
Tel: 01939 220223

gardens on a 320-acre mixed arable farm. Janet and Norman Jones have lived here for 35 years, and for the last ten have offered bed & breakfast accommodation in very comfortable, traditionally appointed bedrooms: a family room and a double with washbasins and fitted showers, and a single. There is a bathroom and a separate toilet. Guests have their own lounge, and excellent breakfasts are served in the beamed dining room. All dietary requirements can be met, including vegan. There's plenty to see and do in the vicinity, including woodland walks and looking over the elaborate ruins of Moreton Corbet Castle; the late-Stuart manor house in the village itself is not open to the public. Grove Farm's owners are happy to provide guests with all the information they need about the local sights.

LOPPINGTON
MAP 2 REF D3
10 miles N of Shrewsbury on the B4397

The manor at Loppington was one of the estates acquired by Judge Jeffreys when he came to Wem. Before this, he had been appointed Lord Chief Justice at the age of 38.

WEM
MAP 2 REF D3
11 miles N of Shrewsbury on the B5476

A peaceful enough place now, but Wem has seen its share of strife, being virtually destroyed in the Wars of the Roses and attacked in the Civil War. On the latter occasion, in 1643, Lord Capel at the head of 5,000 Royalist troops got a pretty hostile reception, and his defeat by a much smaller band, including some townswomen, gave rise to this mocking couplet:

"The women of Wem and a few volunteers
Beat the Lord Capel and all his Cavaliers."

It was another woman – actually a 14-year-old girl called Jane Churm – who nearly did what Capel proved incapable of doing. In setting alight the thatch on the roof of her home she started a fire that destroyed 140 properties in one hour. Some notable buildings survived, including **Astley House**, home of the painter John Astley. This and many of the town's most impressive houses are in **Noble Street**. Famous people associated with Wem include Judge Jeffrey's of Bloody Assize fame, who became Baron Wem in 1685, with his official residence at Lowe Hall. Wem is the home of the modern sweet pea, developed by the 19th-century nurseryman Henry Eckford. **The Sweet Pea Show** and the carnival are great occasions in the Wem calendar.

Darren Sayle, one of the youngest licensees in the country, took over **The White Horse Hotel** in October 1998, continuing the role it began as a coaching stop in the early 17th century. Shoppers, local residents, passers-by and tourists all enjoy the traditional appeal of the bars and lounge. The White Horse also provides overnight accommodation in five letting bedrooms - three doubles, a

The White Horse Hotel, High Street, Wem, Shropshire SY4 5DG
Tel: 01939 232483

twin and a single. Among the other amenities are a games room, a large function room with its own bar, and a beer garden in the courtyard at the back.

WHITCHURCH
MAP 2 REF E2

17 miles N of Shrewsbury on the A49

First developed by the Romans as Mediolanum, Whitchurch is the most important town in the northern part of the county. Its main street is dominated by the tall sandstone tower of **St Alkmund's Church**, in whose chapel lies the body of Sir John Talbot, 1st Earl of Shrewsbury, who was killed at the Battle of Castillon, near Bordeaux, in 1453. **The Shropshire Way** passes nearby, so too the **Llangollen Canal**, and nature-lovers can explore the local wetland habitats – **Brown Moss** is 2 miles to the south off the A41. Whitchurch is the home of **Joyce Clocks**, the oldest tower clockmakers in the world, and is also, somewhat oddly, where Cheshire cheese was created. Hidden away in the heart of the town are the **Old Town Hall Vaults**, where the composer Edward German (*Merrie England, Tom Jones)* was born in 1862. Whitchurch has a major attraction for anglers at **Dearnford Hall Trout Fishery** (Tel: 01948 665914), with fishing from bank or boat, tuition and accommodation.

Georgian and Victorian style rocking horses are the main stock in trade at **The Rocking Horse Workshop**, which is located on the B5476 beside the rounda-

bout where that road meets the A41. David and Noreen Kiss started out at Wem in 1987, and from fairly humble beginnings are now recognised as one of the leading rocking horse manufacturers in the UK. The range of their horses has expanded from two models to a string of over 20, and, in addition, customers can have horses made to their own specification or pattern. David and Noreen use the same traditional methods as their predecessors, from the selection of the timber to the carving, sanding and final touches of hand painting and saddlery. They also undertake the restoration of old rocking horses which have fallen into disrepair, bringing them back to their former glory and putting a shine in the eyes of adoring children - and parents! For DIY restorers, they keep a stock of materials including manes and tails, leatherwork and stirrups. Visitors are welcome to rock up at this magical workshop/showroom, which is open from 9 till 5 Monday to Saturday.

The Rocking Horse Workshop, The Cottage Farm, Tilstock Road, Whitchurch, Shropshire SY13 3JQ Tel: 01948 666777

GRINDLEY BROOK

MAP 2 REF D2

2 miles NW of Whitchurch on the A41

The **Llangollen Canal** runs less than a mile from Whitchurch and at Grindley Brook the famous **staircase locks** are a great attraction.

A mile and a half north of Whitchurch, on the A41 toward Chester and Birkenhead, stands a 300-year-old stone building. This is Richard Crowther's **Lockside Stores**, and within its whitewashed walls is a cornucopia of provisions to meet the needs of walkers, ramblers, motorists and boaters. The last are particularly relevant, as the shop is located at Grindley Brook Locks, a series of six 'staircase' locks which raise and lower the level of the Llangollen Canal, and which, in an area rich in sights and scenery, are an attraction in their own right. Richard keeps a wide and varied stock, from maps, guide books and toiletries to soft drinks, teas and coffees, own-label wines, chilled and frozen food, biscuits

Lockside Stores, Lockside House, Grindley Brook, Near Whitchurch, Shropshire SY13 4QH Tel: 01948 663385

and preserves. His best known speciality is the Welsh oggies, locally made meat pasties of prodigious size that are guaranteed to satisfy the hungriest of hikers. This really useful little place is open April to October, from early in the morning till dusk.

COMBERMERE   MAP 2 REF E2
5 miles N of Whitchurch off the A530

If you are seeking peace, privacy and comfort, look no further - this is the essence of **Combermere Abbey**, whose cottages provide the perfect break from the hustle and bustle of everyday life. The Abbey, which is open for guided tours on Thursdays, is part of an estate dating back 850 years, and at the heart of the estate are 11 individual cottages, each reflecting the personality of its name, as well as the flair of each designer's collection, including Jane Churchill, Ralph Lauren and Nina Campbell; antiques and bespoke furniture complete the picture. The cottages, which each sleep between four and eight, have telephones, colour TVs, videos, CD/tape players, hairdryers, books and games. The kitchens are fully equipped, and a central laundry room has washing machines and dryers. The rooms have either wood-burning fireplaces or coal-effect gas fires, and most of them have private bathrooms or shower rooms. The 17th century library, originally the Abbot's lodge, is used for weddings, concerts and lectures. The philosophy of owner Sarah Callander Beckett and her husband Peter is 'to spoil you, indulge you, and look after you' and the amenities include fishing, swimming in the Mere, cycling (bikes for hire), exploring the lakes and wood-

**Combermere Abbey, Combermere, Near Whitchurch,
Shropshire SY13 4AJ Tel: 01948 871637 Fax: 01948 871293
www.combermereabbey.co.uk e-mail:cottages@combermereabbey.co.uk**

land, or just lying in a hammock watching the world go by. Country suppers, ready to be heated, and Shropshire hampers take the strain out of catering arrangements, and there's a well-stocked larder and shop. All in all, a great place to recharge the batteries, and a perfect antidote to frantic city life. The Abbey stands five miles north of Whitchurch off the A530.

TOURIST INFORMATION CENTRES

Locations in **bold** type are open throughout the year

Herefordshire

Hereford
I King Street, Hereford HR4 9BW
Tel: 01432 268430

Ross-on-Wye
Edde Cross Street, Ross-on-Wye
Tel: 01989 562768

Ledbury
3 The Homend, Ledbury HR8 1BN
Tel: 01531 636147

Leominster
1 Corn Square, Leominster HR6 8LR
Tel: 01568 616460

Bromyard
Heritage Centre, 1 Rowberry Street, Bromyard HR7 4DX
Tel: 01885 482341 (winter) 01885 482038 (summer)

Kington
2 Mill Street, Kington HR5 3BQ
Tel: 01544 230778

Hay-on-Wye
Oxford Road, Hay-on-Wye HR3 5DG
Tel: 01497 820144

Shropshire

Bridgnorth
The Library, Listley Street, Bridgnorth WV16 4AW
Tel: 01746 763257

Church Stretton
Shropshire Hills Information Centre, County Branch Library,
Church Stretton SY6 6DQ Tel: 01694 723133

Ellesmere
Mereside, Ellesmere SY12 0PA
Tel: 01691 622981

Ironbridge
The Wharfage, Ironbridge, Telford TF8 7AW
Tel: 01952 432166

Ludlow
Castle Street, Ludlow SY8 1AS
Tel: 01584 875053

Market Drayton
49 Cheshire Street, Market Drayton TF9 1PH
Tel: 01630 652139

Much Wenlock
The Museum, The Square, Much Wenlock TF13 6HR
Tel: 01952 727679

Oswestry
Mile End, Oswestry SY11 4JA
Tel: 01691 662488

Oswestry
Heritage Centre, 2 Church Terrace, Oswestry SY11 2TE
Tel: 01691 662753

Shrewsbury
The Music Hall, The Square, Shrewsbury SY1 1LH
Tel: 01743 350761

Telford
The Telford Centre, Telford TF3 4XB
Tel: 01952 238008

Whitchurch
Heritage & Information Centre, 12 St Marys Street, Whitchurch SY13 1QY
Tel: 01948 664577

Worcestershire

Bewdley
Load Street, Bewdley DY12 2AE
Tel: 01299 404740

Broadway
1 Cotswold Court, Broadway WR12 7AA
Tel: 01386 852937

Bromsgrove
Bromsgrove Museum, 26 Birmingham Road, Bromsgrove B61 0DD
Tel: 01527 831809

Droitwich Spa
St Richards House, Victoria Square, Droitwich Spa WR9 8DS
Tel: 01905 774312

Evesham
Almonry Museum, Abbey Gate, Evesham WR11 4BG
Tel: 01386 446944

Kidderminster
Severn Valley Railway Station, Comberton Hill, Kidderminster DY10 1QX
Tel: 01562 829400

Malvern
Winter Gardens Complex, Grange Road, Malvern WR14 3HB
Tel: 01684 892289

Pershore
19 High Street, Pershore WR10 1AA
Tel: 01386 554262

Redditch
Civic Square, Alcester Street, Redditch B98 8AH
Tel: 01527 60806

Tenbury Wells
21 Teme Street, Tenbury Wells WR15 8BB
Tel: 01584 810136

Upton-upon-Severn
4 High Street, Upton-upon-Severn WR8 0HB
Tel: 01684 594200

Worcester
The Guildhall, High Street, Worcester WR1 2EY
Tel: 01905 726311

INDEX OF TOWNS, VILLAGES AND PLACES OF INTEREST

Y

INDEX OF PLACES TO STAY, EAT, DRINK & SHOP

THE HIDDEN PLACES
ORDER FORM

To order any of our publications just fill in the payment details below and complete the order form *overleaf*. For orders of less than 4 copies please add £1 per book for postage and packing. Orders over 4 copies are P & P free.

Please Complete Either:

I enclose a cheque for £ .... made payable to Travel Publishing Ltd

Or:

Card No: ☐☐☐☐ ☐☐☐☐ ☐☐☐☐ ☐☐☐☐

Expiry Date: ☐☐☐

Signature: ....

NAME: ....

ADDRESS: ....

....

....

POSTCODE: ....

TEL NO: ....

Please send to: Travel Publishing Ltd
7a Apollo House
Calleva Park
Aldermaston
Berks, RG7 8TN

THE HIDDEN PLACES
ORDER FORM

	Price	Quantity	Value
Regional Titles			
Cambridgeshire & Lincolnshire	£7.99	....	....
Channel Islands	£6.99	....	....
Cheshire	£7.99	....	....
Chilterns	£7.99	....	....
Cornwall	£7.99	....	....
Devon	£7.99	....	....
Dorset, Hants & Isle of Wight	£7.99	....	....
Essex	£7.99	....	....
Gloucestershire	£6.99	....	....
Heart of England	£4.95	....	....
Hereford, Worcs & Shropshire	£7.99	....	....
Highlands & Islands	£7.99	....	....
Kent	£7.99	....	....
Lake District & Cumbria	£7.99	....	....
Lancashire	£7.99	....	....
Norfolk	£7.99	....	....
Northeast Yorkshire	£6.99	....	....
Northumberland & Durham	£6.99	....	....
North Wales	£7.99	....	....
Nottinghamshire	£6.99	....	....
Peak District	£6.99	....	....
Potteries	£6.99	....	....
Somerset	£6.99	....	....
South Wales	£7.99	....	....
Suffolk	£7.99	....	....
Surrey	£6.99	....	....
Sussex	£6.99	....	....
Thames Valley	£7.99	....	....
Warwickshire & West Midlands	£6.99	....	....
Wiltshire	£6.99	....	....
Yorkshire Dales	£6.99	....	....
Set of any 5 Regional titles	**£25.00**	....	....
National Titles			
England	£9.99	....	....
Ireland	£9.99	....	....
Scotland	£9.99	....	....
Wales	£8.99	....	....
Set of all 4 National titles	**£28.00**	....	....
		————	————
		————	————

For orders of less than 4 copies please add £1 per book for postage & packing. Orders over 4 copies P & P free.

THE HIDDEN PLACES
READER COMMENT FORM

The *Hidden Places* research team would like to receive reader's comments on any visitor attractions or places reviewed in the book and also recommendations for suitable entries to be included in the next edition. This will help ensure that the *Hidden Places* series continues to provide its readers with useful information on the more interesting, unusual or unique features of each attraction or place ensuring that their stay in the local area is an enjoyable and stimulating experience.

To provide your comments or recommendations would you please complete the forms below and overleaf as indicated and send to: The Research Department, Travel Publishing Ltd., 7a Apollo House, Calleva Park, Aldermaston, Reading, RG7 8TN.

Your Name:

Your Address:

Your Telephone Number:

Please tick as appropriate: Comments [ ]   Recommendation [ ]

Name of *"Hidden Place"*:

Address:

Telephone Number:

Name of Contact:

THE HIDDEN PLACES
READER COMMENT FORM

Comment or Reason for Recommendation:

....

....

....

....

....

....

....

....

....

....

....

....

THE HIDDEN PLACES
READER COMMENT FORM

The *Hidden Places* research team would like to receive reader's comments on any visitor attractions or places reviewed in the book and also recommendations for suitable entries to be included in the next edition. This will help ensure that the *Hidden Places* series continues to provide its readers with useful information on the more interesting, unusual or unique features of each attraction or place ensuring that their stay in the local area is an enjoyable and stimulating experience.

To provide your comments or recommendations would you please complete the forms below and overleaf as indicated and send to: The Research Department, Travel Publishing Ltd., 7a Apollo House, Calleva Park, Aldermaston, Reading, RG7 8TN.

Your Name:

Your Address:

Your Telephone Number:

Please tick as appropriate: Comments ☐   Recommendation ☐

Name of *"Hidden Place"*:

Address:

Telephone Number:

Name of Contact:

THE HIDDEN PLACES
READER COMMENT FORM

Comment or Reason for Recommendation:

....

....

....

....

....

....

....

....

....

....

....

....

THE HIDDEN PLACES
READER COMMENT FORM

The *Hidden Places* research team would like to receive reader's comments on any visitor attractions or places reviewed in the book and also recommendations for suitable entries to be included in the next edition. This will help ensure that the *Hidden Places* series continues to provide its readers with useful information on the more interesting, unusual or unique features of each attraction or place ensuring that their stay in the local area is an enjoyable and stimulating experience.

To provide your comments or recommendations would you please complete the forms below and overleaf as indicated and send to: The Research Department, Travel Publishing Ltd., 7a Apollo House, Calleva Park, Aldermaston, Reading, RG7 8TN.

Your Name:

Your Address:

Your Telephone Number:

Please tick as appropriate: Comments ☐   Recommendation ☐

Name of *"Hidden Place"*:

Address:

Telephone Number:

Name of Contact:

THE HIDDEN PLACES
READER COMMENT FORM

Comment or Reason for Recommendation:

....

....

....

....

....

....

....

....

....

....

....

....

MAP SECTION

The following pages of maps encompass the main cities, towns and geographical features of Herefordshire, Worcestershire & Shropshire, as well as many of the interesting places featured in the guide. Distances are indicated by the use of scale bars located below each of the maps

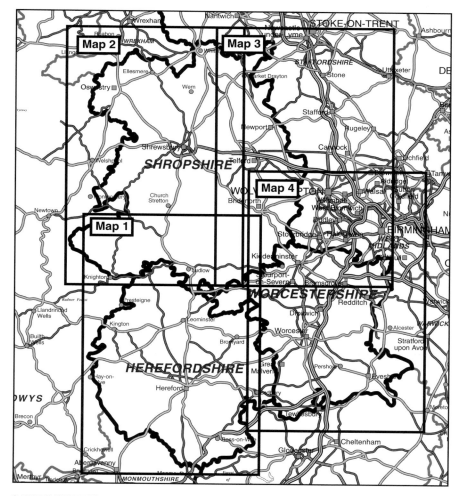

Map 1

2

B   C   D   E   F

Bishop's
Castle

Acton Scott

Aston
Munslow

Ditton
Priors   B4364

Cleobury
North

7

Hopesay

Craven
Arms

B4368

Burwarton

Stoddesdon

Aston-
under-Clun

Clun   Putslow

Stokesay

Onibury

Middleton

A4117

Cleobury
Mortimer

B4364

A4368

Knighton

A4113

Leintwardine

Bromfield

A49

Ludlow

Clee Hill

A456

8

B4355

Brampton Bryan

Wigmore

Richard's
Castle

Orleton

Woofferton

Tenbury
Wells

Whitton

Presteigne

Mortimer's Cross

Ashton

Kimbolton

B4214

9

Radnor Forest

New
Radnor

B4362

Yarpole

B4361

B4203

A44

Walton

Shobdon

Kingsland

Leominster

Edvin Loach

Staunton on Arrow

Eardisland

Monkland

A44

Bromyard Downs

Kington   Pembridge

A44

Stoke Prior

Lyonshall

Dilwyn

Stretford

Hope-under-
Dinmore

Bromyard

4

Almeley

A480

Pencombe

Stanford Bishop

10

A4111

A4112

Weobley

HEREFORDSHIRE

Bishop's
Frome

Whitney-
on-Wye

Eardisley

Kinnersley

Willersley

A4110

A49

Moreton Jeffries

Much Cowarne

A438

Monnington-on-Wye

A438

Sutton St Nicholas

White
Stone

A417

B4214

11

Hay-
on-Wye

Dorstone

Moccas

B4352

Swainshill

Hereford □

Mordiford

A438

Dormington

Peterchurch

B4348

Madley

Coldwell

Holme Lacy

Fownhope

Much Marcle

Kingstone

Abbey Dore

Black

A465

Much Birch

Brockhampton

B4224

A449

B42

12

Ewyas
Harold

Kilpeck

B4348

Hoarwithy

Sellack

How Caple

Yatton

Llanthony

Pontrilas

A466

Bridstow

Mtns.

Michaelchurch

Peterstow

Wilton

4   **3**

Grosmont

Garway

A49

Ross-on-Wye

Crickhowell

Llanvihangel
Crucorney

B4347

Skenfrith

Llanrothal

Whitchurch

Goodrich

Weston-under-Penyard

Mitcheldean

13

A40

B4521

Welsh Newton

A40

A4136

Cinderford

Henvetherine

Symonds Yat

○ Places to Stay, Eat, Drink or Shop

© *MAPS IN MINUTES* ™*1998*

0   5   10   15

Map 2

A B C D E F

Ruabon

Bangor-is-y-coed
B5069
Malpas
A49
A531

A539
WREXHAM
A525
Combermere
A525

2 Llangollen
A5
Overton
Redbrook
Grindley Brook
Whitchurch
Nor

B4500
Glyn Ceiriog
A495
B5476
A41
A529

Ellesmere
Welshampton
Moreton Say

A5
B5063
Ternhill

3 Oswestry
Whittington
A528
Wem
Marchamley

Llanrhaeadr-ym-Mochnant
Loppington
Weston
Hodnet

B4580
Burlton
Preston Brockhurst
A53
A442

Llynclys
Maesbury
Moreton Corbet

Llansantffraid-ym-Mechain
Knockin
B4397
B5476
Preston Gubbals
Shawbury

A49

Llanymynech
A5
Fitz
High Ercall

4 Nesscliffe
Melverley
Withington
Wellington

B4392
Montford

A490
A458
Wollaston
Shrewsbury
A5
7
3

Westbury
B4386
Atcham
Wroxeter
Coalbrookdale

5 A458
Welshpool
B4386
Pontesbury
A458
Ironbridge

A483
Minsterley
Much Wenlock

Forden
A488
SHROPSHIRE
Longnor
Wenlock Edge
B4378

Berriew
Chirbury
Church Stretton
A49
Longville in the Dale

6 Montgomery
A489
Wentnor
B4371

Little Stretton
Ditton Priors

Lydham
Aston Munslow
Cleobury North
Burwarton

Acton Scott
B4368

7 B4368
Bishop's Castle
Hopesay
Craven Arms
B4364

A483
Aston-under-Clun
Puxslow
Stokesay

Clun
A488
Onibury
Middleton
A4117

B4355
Bromfield
A49
Clee Hill

8 A4113
Leintwardine
Ludlow

○ Places to Stay, Eat, Drink or Shop
Brampton Bryan
1

© MAPS IN MINUTES ™ 1998

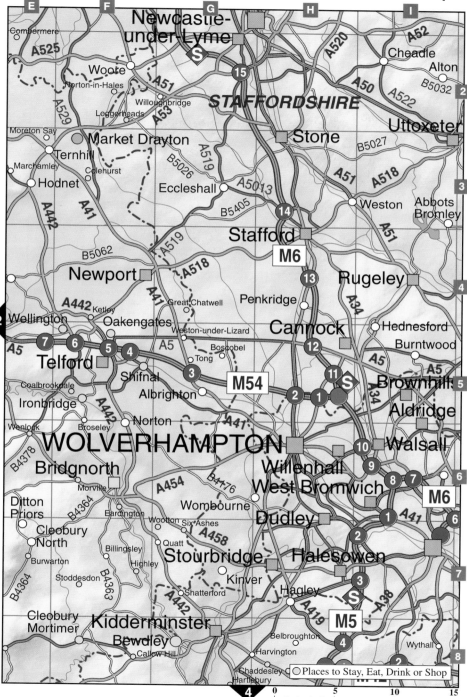

Map 3

Map 4

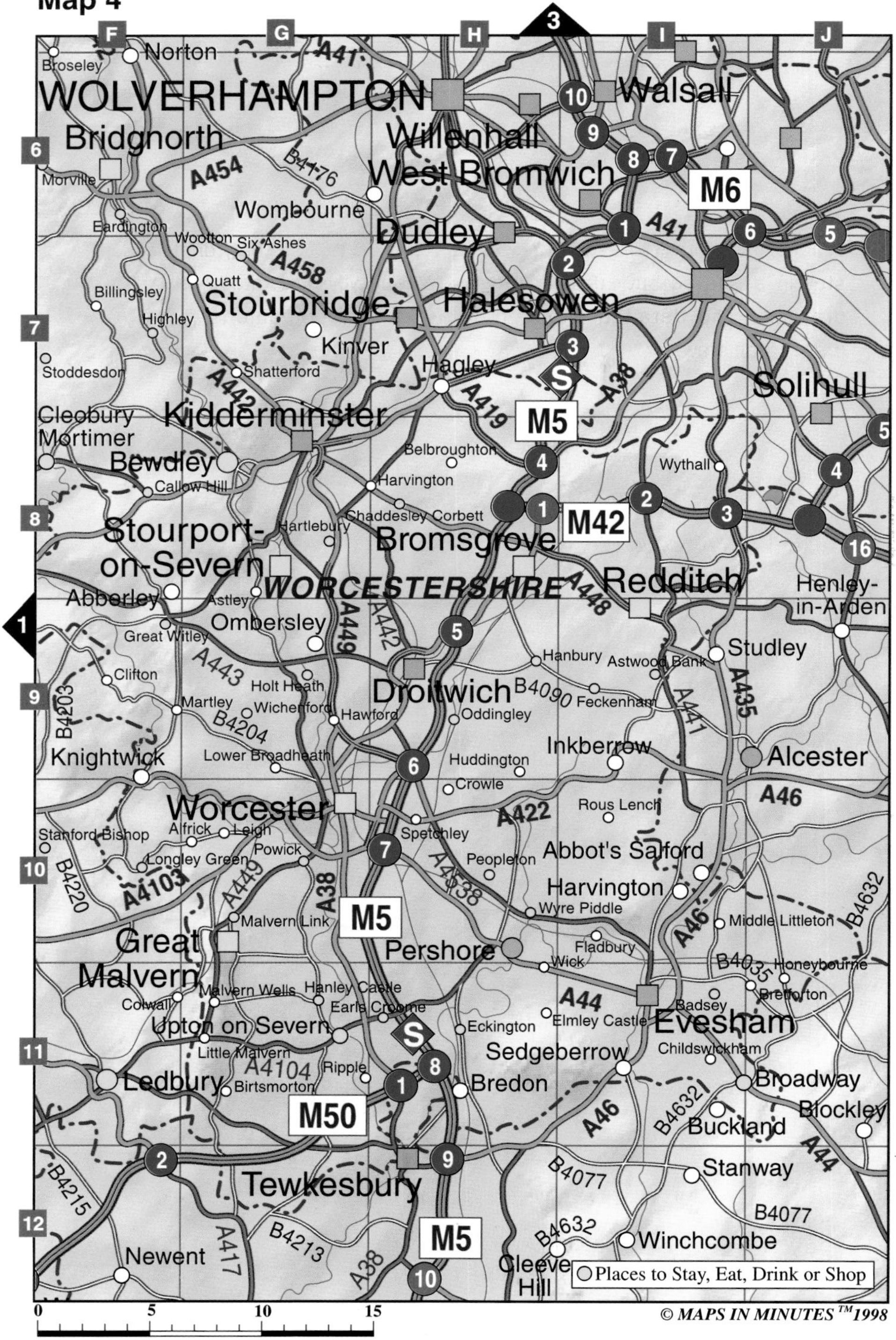

F G 3 H I J

Broseley • Norton

WOLVERHAMPTON

Bridgnorth • Willenhall 10 • **Walsall**

6 Morville • 9

West Bromwich 8 7

Eardington • Wombourne **Dudley** **M6**

Wootton Six Ashes 1 A41

Quatt **Stourbridge** 2 6

Billingsley • **Halesowen** 5

Highley • Kinver 3

Stoddesdon • Shatterford • Hagley **Solihull**

Cleobury Mortimer • S

Bewdley **Kidderminster** **M5** 5

Callow Hill Belbroughton 4 Wythall 4

8 Harvington 2 16

Stourport-on-Severn Shaddesley Corbett 1 **M42** 3

Abberley • Hartlebury **Bromsgrove** Redditch Henley-in-Arden

Great Witley **WORCESTERSHIRE** Studley

Clifton Ombersley 5 Hanbury Astwood Bank

9 B4203 Holt Heath **Droitwich** B4090 Feckenham Alcester

Knightwick Martley Wichenford Hawford Oddingley Inkberrow

Lower Broadheath Huddington A46

Stanford Bishop Alfrick Leigh 6 Crowle Rous Lench

10 Longley Green Powick **Worcester** 7 Spetchley Abbot's Salford

Malvern Link A4103 Peopleton Harvington Middle Littleton

Great Malvern **M5** **Pershore** Wyre Piddle Honeybourne

Colwall Hanley Castle Earls Croome Fladbury Wick Bretforton

Malvern Wells **A44** Badsey

11 Upton on Severn S Eckington Elmley Castle **Evesham**

Little Malvern A4104 Sedgeberrow Childswickham

Ledbury Birtsmorton Ripple 8 Bredon **Broadway** Blockley

1 **M50** Buckland

12 B4215 2 9 Stanway

Tewkesbury B4077 A44

B4213 B4632 B4077

Newent A417 A38 10 Cleeve Hill **Winchcombe**

○ Places to Stay, Eat, Drink or Shop

0 5 10 15

© *MAPS IN MINUTES* ™ 1998